What people are saying about

The Irish Pagan Book of Rites

The Irish Book of Rites is unique, a dual language text that offers evocative rituals in both English and Irish. A wonderful way to connect to your spirituality across the tides of the year; truly something that all Irish pagans should have on their shelf. **Morgan Daimler**, author of *Irish Paganism* and *Gods and Goddesses of Ireland*

The author has done an incredible amount of research into traditions and folklore to bring us a beautifully written book on Irish Pagan prayers and rites of all kinds. Fascinating to read and very useful to work with, including the use of dual language. Very impressive.
Rachel Patterson, Witch and author of *The Cailleach*, *Beneath the Moon* and *Witchcraft into the Wilds*

John McLoughlin has created a much needed Pagan Irish devotional based in genuine Irish culture and history that will be of interest to anyone with ancestry from the far flung Irish and Celtic diaspora, world-wide. A book like this one should be required reading for any aspiring Druid or Celtic Pagan who seeks to perform rituals based in ancient tradition. I will certainly be recommending it to my students.
Ellen Evert Hopman, Archdruid of Tribe of the Oak (www.tribeoftheoak.com) and author of the *Druid trilogy* of novels, of *A Legacy of Druids – Conversations with Druid leaders of Britain, the USA and Canada, past and present, A Druid's Herbal of Sacred Tree Medicine, Tree Medicine Tree Magic,* and other volumes

In this beautiful collection of rites, McLoughlin has worked hard to preserve not only the traditions of pagan Ireland, but the original language in which they would have been performed. While the English versions lend flexibility to modern readers, the Irish renditions really bring out the joy and reverence so essential to effective spiritual practice.

Logan Albright, author of *Libertarian Paganism* and *Conform or Be Cast Out: The (Literal) Demonization of Nonconformists*

Pagan Portals
The Irish Pagan Book of Rites

Rituals and Prayers for Daily Life
and Festivals

Do mo bhuimí choimhdeachta
Mary, Carolyn & Joan

Pagan Portals
The Irish Pagan Book of Rites

Rituals and Prayers for Daily Life
and Festivals

John Michael McLoughlin

MOON
BOOKS
Winchester, UK
Washington, USA

JOHN HUNT PUBLISHING

First published by Moon Books, 2024
Moon Books is an imprint of John Hunt Publishing Ltd., No. 3 East Street, Alresford
Hampshire SO24 9EE, UK
office@jhpbooks.net
www.johnhuntpublishing.com
www.moon-books.net

For distributor details and how to order please visit the 'Ordering' section on our website.

ISBN: 978 1 80341 476 8
978 1 80341 477 5 (ebook)
Library of Congress Control Number: 2022952110

A CIP catalogue record for this book is available from the British Library.

Design: Lapiz Digital Services

UK: Printed and bound by CPI Group (UK) Ltd, Croydon, CR0 4YY
Printed in North America by CPI GPS partners

We operate a distinctive and ethical publishing philosophy in
all areas of our business, from our global network of authors to
production and worldwide distribution.

Contents

Introduction

This book is an offering. It is foremost an offering to the Gods who set the spark of life in my bones, the cool lake air of my home in my lungs, and the fire of inspiration in my head. It is an offering to my Ancestors, upon whose shoulders I struggle to stand, whose perseverance and example supports me and drives me forward. It is an offering to the abundant, nurturing Land upon which I walk, whose life-giving food and water sustains me, whose beauty constantly inspires me, whose forests of trees and crystal blue lakes shelter and invigorate me. To them is given all thanks and the outpouring of these devotions of the heart, that others may rediscover their place at the fire alongside their Ancestors, a place amid the stones, between Earth, Sea, and Sky.

le sochar dár n-anam is gcoirp, dár gcairde is ngaolta, le neartú na nDéithe agus le cóir na saolta.

for the benefit of our souls and bodies, for our friends and family, for the strengthening of the Gods and the right order of the worlds.

These pages contain a collection of rites and prayers to the ancestral Gods and Goddesses of the Irish people. This includes a main rite, or *deasghnáth*, for regularly made offerings which can be made solitary or in fellowship with others. Additionally, there are included rites for the blessing of lustral water, the blessing of a house, and celebrations for the four main festivals of the traditional Irish year.

The texts of these ceremonies have been harvested from many sources, from ancient Irish texts such as the *Lebor Gabhala na hErin* (Book of the Invasions of Ireland), the *Táin Bó Cuailnge* (the Cattle-Raid of Cooley), the *Suigidud Tellaich Temra* (the

1

Settling of the Manor of Tara), a myriad of folk accounts, and from the creativity of my own pen.

We have few surviving works from the age when our Ancestors worshiped their indigenous traditions, and some may question the authenticity or appropriateness of using texts compiled by Christians and/or outright used in Christian prayer.

It is true we have painfully little in the form of texts and nothing of liturgy from pre-Christian Ireland. Let us, however, take confidence in a fact of history: as with most of Europe, it was not Ireland that converted to Christianity, so much as Christianity that converted to Ireland. The sacred wells and rivers never lost their sanctity, but rather swapped the native names of our Gods and Goddesses for those of saints. The Gods and Ancestors never left their holy mounds and stone circles, nor was the awesome reverence lost which the people held for these places. Names changed. Stories became masked, perhaps distorted but not destroyed. Most especially, the monolithic male deity of the Abrahamic religions could in no way deter the intense devotion of the Irish people for their Goddesses, and this ancient love endured and thrived in the characteristically Irish fervor for the Virgin Mary and her many aspects, and for Saint Brigid and other Goddesses who have worn the masks of saints for the past several centuries. Finally, right up to our times the hills are lit with bonfires at Bealtaine and Oíche Shamhna (1st May and 1st November, respectively), festivals which centuries of priestly preaching and interdicts could do nothing to deter.

Therefore, we can offer these prayers and the surviving lore with greater confidence, knowing that beneath and even through the veneer of the Christian centuries, the deep and rich inheritance of our native spirituality endures. The indigenous ways of the Ancestors were not suddenly severed at the coming of Saint Patrick. Far from it. The Gods and Goddesses of Éire are alive and well, and we are the inheritors of an ancestral fire which the cross could not extinguish. May the pages of this book be as the passing of that fire from my hearth to yours, and together we shall see it blaze.

1

Preparatory Rites

It can be a good idea to prepare before any big undertaking. Whether it's the athlete doing stretches before the race, or the singer performing warm-up exercises, these preparations can help place us in the right state of mind and ensure the best performance. The spiritual realm is no different, and while these exercises aren't necessary, they can be incredibly helpful in clearing the mind, enhancing focus, and grounding one's intentions.

What follows are two devotionals. As with all the rites in this book, they may be performed alone or in a group. These may be done prior to the main *deasghnáth* or at any time on their own as a means of purification and grounding. They are the *deasghnáth ionnalta* (rite of purification) and *na Trí Neimheadh* (the Three Holies).

Deasghnáth Ionnalta ~ Rite of Purification

Life isn't easy. Despite our best efforts and intentions, plans fall through, emotions run high, feelings get hurt, and connections fall apart. Most of us journey the winding spiral path of life through this world at the mercy of powers and structures beyond our control, exerting themselves all around us, pushing and pulling us, our friends and family this way and that. We ride from peaks of joy to valleys of despair, and while the spiritually minded of us yearn for a respite and meaning amid these trials, we constantly fail to meet even our own expectations, and we disappoint and hurt others.

We are not "fallen" creatures, once perfect and now lost, nor are we prone to sin. We simply *are*. Through lives of conscious living, striving to set our little corners of the universe in right order, we can each take a step towards greater *cóir* in the cosmos. *Cóir* is an immense word containing within it the sense of justice, equity, and setting things aright. This Rite of Purification provides us a symbolic, spiritual way to cleanse ourselves of our attachments to all those many failings, faults, harms and hurts which we have endured or done to others, and to move forward in our commitment to set things right.

If a person has intentionally harmed another by word or deed, they should do their best to rectify the situation with that person before performing this rite. We have no sort of "confession" to wipe away the consequences and guilt of one's actions. In our Ancestral ways, each individual is responsible for their actions; and indeed, traditionally the consequences of one's deeds are seen as extending to one's whole family and other relationships, reminding us that we are all connected, and must act virtuously not only for our own sake, but for the sake of our friends and family as well.

Deasghnáth Ionnalta ~ Rite of Purification

Pouring water over palms:

Ionnlaim do bhosa
Ann sna fhrasa fíona
Ann sa lí na lasa
Ann sna seacht síonta
Ann sa tsubh craoibhe
Ann sa bhainne meala
Is cuirim na naoi mbuanna glana caoine
ann do cheann caomh geal:

Making a pour of water over the head for each virtue:

Bua crutha
Bua gutha
Bua ratha
Bua maithe
Bua críonnachta
Bua féile
Bua rogha finne
Bua an fíor-oireachtais
Bua an dea-labhra

Deasghnáth Ionnalta ~ Rite of Purification

Pouring water over palms:

I bathe your palms
In the streams of wine
In the luster of fire
In the seven elements
In the juice of raspberries
In the milk of honey
And I place the nine pure keen virtues
upon your fair fond face:

Making a pour of water over the head for each virtue:

Virtue of form
Virtue of voice
Virtue of abundance
Virtue of goodness
Virtue of wisdom
Virtue of generosity
Virtue of choice fairness
Virtue of true-loveliness
Virtue of goodly speech.

Lighting a taper or candle:

Is dubh an domhan thall úd
Is dubh na daoine ansiúd

Circling around with the flame:

Is tusa an eala dhonn
Tá dul isteach chun cinn

Presenting candle towards the heart:

Tá a gcroíthe faoi do chonn

Presenting candle towards the lips:

Tá a dteanga faoi do bhonn

Placing the candle in the hands:

Is ar chaoi cha ndéarfaidh siad aon
focal is oil leat.

Lighting a taper or candle:

Dark is the world beyond
Dark are the people therein

Circling around with the flame:

You are the brown swan
Going in among them

Presenting candle towards the heart:

Their hearts are under your control

Presenting candle towards the lips:

Their tongues are under your sole

Placing the candle in the hands:

Nor will they ever utter
a word of offense against you.

Anointing with oil or lustral water the forehead:

Is dobhar ar teas thú
Is seascair ar fuacht thú
Is súile don dhall thú
Is crann don dheoraí trua
Is oileán ar muir thú
Is caiseal ar tír thú
Is fuarán san fhásach thú
Is sláinte don thé atá tinn.

Raising hands in blessing:

Bíodh fáilte mar an Daghda agat
Bíodh beos mar na Brighid agat
Bíodh neart mar na Morrigan agat
Bíodh eolas mar an Lugh agat
Bíodh cumhacht mar an Manannán agat
Bíodh brí mar an Aongus agat
Bíodh leigheas mar an Dian Céacht agat
Bíodh eagna mar na Sinsir an dúchais agat.

Anointing with oil or lustral water the forehead:

A shade are you in the heat
A shelter are you in the cold
Eyes are you to the blind
A tree to the wretched wanderer
An island are you in the sea
A fortress are you on land
A spring are you in the desert
Health to those who are ill.

Raising hands in blessing:

May the joy of the Daghda be yours
May the liveliness of Brigid be yours
May the strength of the Morrigan be yours
May the knowledge of Lugh be yours
May the power of Manannán be yours
May the vigor of Aongus be yours
May the healing of Dian Céacht be yours
May the wisdom of the Ancestors of the old ways be yours.[1]

Purified individual now recites, singularly or with others, the Dán Aimheirgín (the Song of Amergin):

Mé gaoth ar muir
Mé tonn díleann
Mé fuaim mara
Mé damh seacht mbeann
Mé seabhac den aill
Mé dealán gréine
Mé caoine luibhe
Mé torc ar ghail
Mé heo i linn
Mé loch i má
Mé brí na ndéithe
Mé brí dána
Mé brí i bhfodhbh fras feochadh
Mé dia a dheilbheas do cheann connadh

Cé hé a mhíníos clochar sléibhe?
Cé hé a áirmhíos trátha éasca?
Cé do is eol cá bhfuineann grian?

Purified individual now recites, singularly or with others, the Dán
Aimheirgín (the Song of Amergin):

I am the wind on the sea
I am the wave of the sea
I am the voice of the sea
I am the bull of seven battles
I am the eagle on the rock
I am a flash from the sun
I am the most beautiful of plants
I am a strong wild boar
I am a salmon in the water
I am a lake in the plain
I am the word of the gods
I am the word of knowledge
I am the head of the spear in battle
I am the god that puts fire in the head

Who spreads light in the gathering on the hills?
Who can tell the ages of the moon?
Who can tell the place where the sun rests?[2]

Na Trí Neimheadh ~ The Three Holies

This last of the preparatory rites is the shortest, but within its brevity provides immense space for personal grounding and calming meditation. We stand amid the three sacred realms of Earth, Sea and Sky, now cleansed and separated physically, mentally and spiritually from the mundane order and standing on the threshold of the numinous.

We reach our hands to the sky, we breathe in deeply from the abdomen, and say, *"Neamh os ár gcionn* (sky above us)."

We then bend respectfully and touch our hands to the earth, exhaling, and say, *"Talamh faoi bhun* (earth beneath)."

Lastly, standing back upright, we stretch our arms out to the sides and slowly bring them in as though an embrace, ending with palms crossed over the heart, saying, *"Muir timpeall orainn* (sea around us)."

We recite this simple meditation three times, seeing ourselves standing amid and connecting to the entire cosmos in its sacred and ancient tripartite emanation as Earth, Sea and Sky. This rite, whether in full form or simply as a *mantra* accompanying breathing for meditation, may be used at any time to ground and center oneself.

2

Deasghnáth an Neimhidh
The Rite of the Grove

Grounded and purified, we are now ready to honor the Land, the Ancestors, and the Gods. The fundamental rite is called the *deasghnáth an neimhidh*, that is, the "rite of the grove". The Irish word *deasghnáth* is a compound of two words, *deas* "correct/rightward/sunwise/lucky" and *gnáth* "custom/habit". The word *neimhidh* is the genitive form of the word *neimheadh* which means "sanctuary/holy thing". *Neimheadh* has ancient roots, recognizable back to ancient Gaul in its word *nemeton* used for the sacred groves of the druids.

Like the druids of old, we continue to gather in groves, taking our place within an ancestral tradition whose roots reach deep into the unrecorded mists of time. Many prefer to make their offerings out in the open, in a natural space beneath open sky and trees with soil beneath our feet. We are not limited by physical space, however, and these rites may be offered in any place that is well maintained and does honor to the Gods. The sacred grove may be a woodland clearing as in ancestral times, or just as well be one's living room, bedroom, or hotel room. This rite recognizes the inherent sacredness of the natural world while also providing the opportunity and words to sanctify whatever place we find ourselves in. Fundamentally, by realigning ourselves with the Gods, with our Ancestors, with the good spirits of the Land, we place ourselves in right order with the worlds, and assert with our words and actions the power to make holy again what has otherwise become corrupted by the forgetfulness of the unbalanced world.

Why Do We Make Offering?

The making of offerings to our Gods is so widespread in human cultures across time and space that we might very well conclude that it is something inherent, even instinctual. The common traits of all human societies have been the acknowledgment of the Gods, seeing the need to make offering to them, and to make that offering by way of sacrifice. We are truly *homo sacrificiens*.

The reasons for this are manifold. There is something inherent in humanity that yearns for the Gods, for the numinous *other* which moves the universe and which radiates forth from the wondrous world all around us. Since our first steps we humans have danced with spirits. We saw them in the brilliant sun and moon, the twinkling stars, the wind which emerges unknown to cool as well as with power to destroy, the furious storm, played with them in the nourishing rain, under the sheltering trees, and knew them in the many animals and insects with whom we share our home. Our first instinct is to see and meet these awesome *others* and to give them thanks for the goods they give us, to adore that which is beautiful or mysterious, to supplicate them out of desire for further goods to be received or dangers averted, and to make reparation for wrongs we may have done to them or to others.

We can sum up and remember the four main purposes of offering with the handy acronym *A.R.T.S.*

> **Adoration** – We may offer out of adoration and awe of the Gods, love for our Ancestors, and respect for the Land beneath and all around us.
> **Reparation** – We may offer out of regret or sorrow for wrongs done against the Gods, for faults committed against others, or for atrocities done against the Land.
> **Thanksgiving** – We may make an offering of thanks for the goodness which the Gods have bestowed upon us, for the

life and ways the Ancestors gave us, and for the abundance of the Earth.

Supplication – We may make our offerings as a way of asking the divine for some goodness or blessing we wish to see manifest.

Our offerings may be specifically for one of these intentions, or may include several or all of them. The words of the *deasghnáth an neimhidh* embodies all of these.

Ritual Objects

The *deasghnáth an neimhidh* assumes the use of a few things for the ritual. None of these are essential, except that which is offered itself, though a minimalist rite would do well to at least have a sort of flame present (such as a candle).

The full rite includes:

Altar – This may take many forms. An altar may be as simple as a spot on a table or the ground, a pile of stones, or an elaborate pillar or wooden structure upon which the offering and other ritual objects are set. Regardless, it should be treated as a place and object of respect.

Fire – Ideally a fire in a fire-pit or hearth. The fire should have a central place in the Grove, or be placed in the east to symbolize the rising sun or the south to symbolize the direction of heat and the noonday sun (alternatively, placed in the north for individuals in the southern hemisphere).

Lustral Water – This is water from a natural source which has been blessed for ritual use.

Offering Bowl – This is a bowl sufficiently large enough to contain any offerings without spilling or dropping. For some rituals or kinds of offerings, a bowl may not be necessary or practical, and it is fine to use the bowl for some offerings (e.g. libations), while having other offerings off to the side or on the altar (e.g. a loaf of bread).

Ogham – These are pieces of wood or stones with ogham script etched upon them and may be used for divination. It is a good practice to divine if the offering was accepted after it was made. This is not essential if a person does not have ogham or chooses not to incorporate them. Other forms of divination, such as runes, may be used as well.

Deasghnáth an Neimhidh ~ The Rite of the Grove

Croitheadh uisce naofa

The celebrant takes the lustral water and stands before the central part of the grove.

Gairim ar Talamh, ar Muir is ar Neamh, teacht i gcúnamh orainn. (*sprinkles the ground, altar and air above with lustral water*)

Sprinkling towards each direction named:

Thoir bláth
Theas séis
Thiar fios
Thuaidh cath
In idirmheán flaith[3]

Sprinkling the grove clockwise, the celebrant says:

Go naomhaítear duit, a Fhiodhneimhidh Naofa,
an áit a gcónaíonn na Dea-Dhúile na Tíre seo.
Go naomhaítear daoibh, go naomhaítear daoibh,
go naomhaítear daoibh, agus go raibh dea-aigne eadrainn.

During the above prayer, a small offering appropriate to the land spirits may be poured or set out on the ground to the north. Milk or cream are ideal, neutral offerings.

Deasghnáth an Neimhidh ~ The Rite of the Grove

Sprinkling of lustral water

The celebrant takes the lustral water and stands before the central part of the grove.

I call upon Earth, upon Sea and Sky, to come to our aid. (*sprinkles the ground, altar and air above with lustral water*)

Sprinkling towards each direction named:

Prosperity in the east
Music in the south
Knowledge in the west
Battle in the north
Sovereignty in the center

Sprinkling the grove clockwise, the celebrant says:

May you be blessed, O Sacred Holy Grove,
the place where dwell the Good Spirits of this Land.
May you be blessed, may you be blessed,
may you be blessed, and may there be good-will between us.

During the above prayer, a small offering appropriate to the land spirits may be poured or set out on the ground to the north. Milk or cream are ideal, neutral offerings.

Lasadh na tine ~ Lighting of the fire

The celebrant or other participant lights the central fire.

Tógaim an tine seo
i láthair na Dea-Dhúl na Tíre seo,
i láthair na Sinsear
i láthair na nDéithe
gan fiarán, gan danartha, gan díomas,
agus i measc na dTrí Neimheadh dár dtearmann

The celebrant raises fire or, having lit a taper or lamp from the hearth, raises it towards the west, praying the following while walking clockwise around the grove with the light.

Tagaigí agus bígí linn, a Shinsir dhil gheal!
Céad fáilte romhaibh, a Aithreacha is a Mháithreacha,
A Sheanaithreacha is a Sheanmháithreacha,
Le ríomh siar go tosach aimsire.
Beannaímid daoibh, a ghaolta dhil
agus go mbeannaí sibh dúinn
le bheith ag gardáil ár n-anamacha is ár gcoirp,
anois agus inár gcruachás.
Míle altú buí libh as bhur gcabhair is gcion,
agus míle fáilte romhaibh go dtí an neimheadh.

Now an offering may be poured out or set upon the ground in the west for the Ancestors. Milk, cream, butter, porridge, ale, mead, beer, liquor, various meats, vegetables or fruits are all appropriate offerings.

Lasadh na tine ~ Lighting of the fire

The celebrant or other participant lights the central fire.

I kindle this fire
in the presence of the good spirits of this land
in the presence of the Ancestors
in the presence of the Gods
without petulance, without cruelty, without arrogance,
and amid the Three Holies for our refuge.

The celebrant raises fire or, having lit a taper or lamp from the hearth, raises it towards the west, praying the following while walking clockwise around the grove with the light.

Come and be with us, beloved Ancestors!
A hundred welcomes to you, Fathers and Mothers,
Grandfathers and Grandmothers,
Stretching back to the beginning of time.
We bless you, dearest kin
and may you bless us,
guarding our souls and our bodies,
now and in time of distress.
A thousand thanks to you for your assistance and love,
and a thousand welcomes to you to the grove.

Now an offering may be poured out or set upon the ground in the west for the Ancestors. Milk, cream, butter, porridge, ale, mead, beer, liquor, various meats, vegetables or fruits are all appropriate offerings.

Achainí ar na Déithe ~ Invocation of the Gods

Before the altar or central fire, facing east or towards the fire, the celebrant says the invocations aloud and with hands raised.

Molaimid daoibh, a Dhéithe Dhílse Mholfacha,
Go mbeannaítear daoibh idir Talaimh, Muir, is Neamh,
agus go n-éiste sibh ár nglór nuair a ngairimid oraibh:

Following are a series of short invocations which may be used for some of the highest and most often called-upon Gods and Goddesses. The celebrant is welcome to use their own words, or the silent unspoken call of their own heart instead. The celebrant says these invocations aloud and with hands raised in welcome.
There is a common practice to invoke Manannán mac Lir first. He lays the féth fíada, *the mist of invisibility, over the Gods and their dwellings, and so we ask him to lift the veil, opening the gates between us and the numinous other to receive our offering. One may invoke as many deities by name as desired, or choose to go right to the invocation for all the Gods.*

Manannán mac Lir

A Mhanannáin
A Oirbsiu
A Mhac Lir

A thiarnaíonn do na mara móra
Agus a osclaíonn na geataí idir an saol seo agus an saol eile,
Tóg d'fhéth fíada de, agus bí linn cois na tine seo.

An Dagda

A Dhagda
A Eochaid Ollathair
A Ruadh Ro-Fessa

A dtugann do Lorga Mhór beatha is bás,
Agus nach n-imíonn a choire aon duine neamhshásta as,
Bí linn cois na tine seo.

Achaíní ar na Déithe ~ Invocation of the Gods

Before the altar or central fire, facing east or towards the fire, the celebrant says the invocations aloud and with hands raised.

We praise you, O Faithful and Mighty Gods,
May you be blessed amid Earth, Sea, and Sky,
and may you hear our voice as we call upon you:

Following are a series of short invocations which may be used for some of the highest and most often called-upon Gods and Goddesses. The celebrant is welcome to use their own words, or the silent unspoken call of their own heart instead. The celebrant says these invocations aloud and with hands raised in welcome.

There is a common practice to invoke Manannán mac Lir first. He lays the féth fíada, *the mist of invisibility, over the Gods and their dwellings, and so we ask him to lift the veil, opening the gates between us and the numinous other to receive our offering. One may invoke as many deities by name as desired, or choose to go right to the invocation for all the Gods.*

Manannán mac Lir

A Mhanannáin
A Oirbsiu
A Mhac Lir

Who rules over the great seas
Who opens the gates between this world and the Otherworld
Lift your mist of invisibility, and be with us by this fire.

An Dagda

A Dhagda
A Eochaid Ollathair
A Ruadh Ro-Fessa

Whose mighty club bestows life and death
and from whose cauldron goes none away unsatisfied,
be with us by this fire.

An Morrígan

A Mhorrígan
A Mhacha
A Bhadhbh

A fhaigheann bua thar ár naimhde
Tar agus cuidigh linn i gach cathú dá bhfuilimid ann,
agus bí linn cois na tine seo.

Brigid

A Bhríd
A Ní-Dhagda
A Tine Tinfidh

Leath orainn do bhrat
Tú lasair an-mhór na heagna sa dorchadas.
Bí linn cois na tine seo.

Lugh

A Lugh
A Lámhfhada
A Ildánach

Cosain sinn agus cuir cath as ár n-ucht,
mar a throid tú as ucht na nDéithe agus a sheachain tú do
mhacsa ina scís.
Bí linn cois na tine seo.

Aongus

A Aongus
A Mhac Óg
A Mhac Daghda

A rinne nithiúil an grá in aisling amharctha,
Agus a chuireann i gcrích fíor-dhúil an chroí,
Bí linn cois na tine seo.

An Morrígan

A Mhorrígan
A Mhacha
A Bhadhbh

Who grants victory over our enemies:
Come and aid us in every struggle we are in,
and be with us by this fire.

Brigid

A Bhríd
A Ní-Dhagda
A Tine Tinfidh

Spread your mantle over us
You, great fire of wisdom in the darkness.
Be with us by this fire.

Lugh

A Lugh
A Lámhfhada
A Ildánach

Guard us and do battle for us,
as you fought on behalf of the Gods and shielded your son in
his weariness.
Be with us by this fire.

Aongus

A Aongus
A Mhac Óg
A Mhac Daghda

Who made real the love of your vision,
and manifests the heart's true love and desire,
be with us by this fire.

Nuada

A Nuada
A Airgeadláimh
A Rí is Airde

A láimhsíonn an claíomh solais mar rí na dTuath Dé Danann
agus a chosnaíonn do mhuintir le d'Airgeadlámh,
Bí linn cois na tine seo.

Dian Cécht

A Dian Cécht
A Lia na nDéithe
A Mhac Dagda

A leigheasann neach saolta is neamhshaolta i do Thobar Sláine
Agus a shlánaíonn an lámh Nuadha agus an tsúil Midhir as do
leigheas,
Bí linn cois na tine seo.

Ogma

A Ogma
A Thréainfhir
A Ghrianaineach

File deaslabhartha i measc na nDéithe
a chruthaigh an oghamchraobh agus a ndeir a chlaíomh Orna
an fhírinne,
Bí linn cois na tine seo.

Na Déithe uile ~ All the Gods

Gairim ar na Déithe Uile Ró-Naofa,
Na Déithe Buacha na Talún, Mara, is Neimhe,
Na Déithe ár Sinsear ó thosach aimsire.
Bí linn cois na tine seo.

Nuada

A Nuada
A Airgeadláimh
A Rí is Airde

Who wields the Sword of Light as King of the Tuatha Dé Danann
and who protects your people with your Silver Arm,
Be with us by this fire.

Dian Cécht

A Dian Cécht
A Lia na nDéithe
A Mhac Dagda

Who heals every worldly and Otherworldly being in your Well
of Sláine
and makes whole the arm of Nuadha and the eye of Midhir by
your remedy,
be with us by this fire.

Ogma

A Ogma
A Thréainfhir
A Ghrianaineach

Eloquent poet among the Gods
who creates the ogham-script and whose sword Orna speaks
the truth,
Be with us by this fire.

Na Déithe uile ~ All the Gods

I call upon the All the Most Holy Gods,
The Victorious Gods of Earth, Sea, and Sky,
The Gods of our Ancestors from the beginning of time.
Be with us by this fire.

Ullmhú Íobartha ~ Preparation for Offering

The celebrant spreads lustral water over the hands and then dabs the forehead, mouth, and heart with the water, saying:

A Dhéithe ionúine, toirbhrím mé féin daoibh leis an íobairt seo. A Shinsir a mhilse mo chroí, tagaigí i gcabhair orm, i gcruth go n-onóraímid na Déithe go fiúntach, d'fhonn is go bhfaighimid a mbeannachtaí.

An Íobairt ~ The Offering

The celebrant takes offering and sets it on or just in front of or to the side of the altar. It is not yet poured out. With hands raised, the celebrant prays the following on behalf of friends and family:

A Dhéithe Ionúine is Mholfacha,
ofrálaimid na hurnaithe is íobairt seo
mar a d'ordaigh ár Sinsir romhainn
le sochar dár n-anamacha is gcoirp,
dár gcairde is ngaolta,
le neartú na nDéithe
agus le cóir na saolta.

Neart ár Sinsir, bígí dár neart anois,
inniu agus gach oíche is lá atá le teacht.
Go stiúra sibh
Go naomhaí sibh
agus go gcosnaí sibh
sinn, ár muintir, agus go háirithe mo Chlann (list personal family names)
agus mo chairde is mo ghaolta (list names of people you especially wish to pray for).

Go neartaí an íobairt seo sibh
Go nglaca sibh leis an íobairt seo ónár lámha
Chun ard-onóra s'agaibhse.

Ullmhú Íobartha ~ Preparation for Offering

The celebrant spreads lustral water over the hands and then dabs the forehead, mouth, and heart with the water, saying:

O Beloved Gods, I dedicate myself to you with this offering.
O dearest Ancestors of my heart, come to my assistance, that we may honor the Gods worthily,
so that we may receive their blessings.

An Íobairt ~ The Offering

The celebrant takes offering and sets it on or just in front of or to the side of the altar. It is not yet poured out. With hands raised, the celebrant prays the following on behalf of friends and family:

O Gods Beloved and Mighty,
we offer these prayers and this sacrifice
as our Ancestors before us ordained
for the benefit of our souls and bodies,
for our friends and family,
for the strengthening of the Gods
and the right order of the worlds.

Strength of our Ancestors, be our strength now,
today and every night and day to come.
May you guide
May you bless
and may you protect
us, our people, and especially my Clan (list personal family names)
and my friends and my family (list names of people you especially want to pray for).

May this offering strengthen you
May you accept this offering from our hands
to your high-honor.

Naomhú an Íobartaigh ~ Hallowing of the Offering

If a liquid oblation, the celebrant now takes the container of it and circles it clockwise over the altar three times for each verse of the following prayer. If the grove allows, the celebrant may walk around the grove holding the offering aloft for each verse. At the conclusion of each verse, the celebrant raises the container towards the altar or fire and then pours out some of the offering into the offering bowl, and then — if able and the substance is drinkable — takes a sip of it as well. The same is done for other offerings, though if large they are not carried, but rather the celebrant — and those attending — may walk around the offering itself while saying the prayer, and then place the right hand upon it at the end of each verse.

Neart fiaigh duibh daoibh
Neart iolair daoibh
Neart dreoilín

Neart toirní daoibh
Neart gealaí daoibh
Neart gréine

Neart talún daoibh
Neart mara daoibh
Neart neimhe

Naomhú an Íobartaigh ~ Hallowing of the Offering

If a liquid oblation, the celebrant now takes the container of it and circles it clockwise over the altar three times for each verse of the following prayer. If the grove allows, the celebrant may walk around the grove holding the offering aloft for each verse. At the conclusion of each verse, the celebrant raises the container towards the altar or fire and then pours out some of the offering into the offering bowl, and then — if able and the substance is drinkable — takes a sip of it as well. The same is done for other offerings, though if large they are not carried, but rather the celebrant — and those attending — may walk around the offering itself while saying the prayer, and then place the right hand upon it at the end of each verse.

The strength of the raven be with you
The strength of the eagle be with you
The strength of the wren

The strength of the thunder be with you
The strength of the moon be with you
The strength of the sun

The strength of the earth be with you
The strength of the sea be with you
The strength of the sky

An Doirteadh ~ The Pouring-out

Placing the right hand over or upon the offering, the celebrant prays:

A Dhéithe,
de réir dúchais ár Sinsir ofráilimid sibh an íobairt seo.
Go naomhaí sibh
Go nglaca sibh
Go gcaithe sibh
an rogha íobartaigh seo.

The offering is poured out into the fire or onto the earth. A small amount should remain in the offering bowl for the blessing—if occurring—and for the éiric. Meanwhile the following is declared:

Mar a thugtar, mar a ghabhtar,
agus tugtar daoibh ar ais.

After all offerings have been poured out save for a small amount for subsequent blessings and the éiric, the celebrant continues:

Go dtuga an bheatha an íobartaigh seo beatha daoibh, a Dhéithe Chumhachtacha,
go neartaí sí sibh agus go móra sí sibh.

Go naomhaítear na saolta uile as an naofacht na híobartha seo, agus go neartaí sé ár Sinsir is ár Mairbh Mhuirneacha, go háirithe (*list names of particular beloved dead*).
Go dtuga sibh áthas is suaimhneas dóibh, go bhfeicfimid arís iad agus rachaimid in aoibhneas leo.

Is naomhaítear sibh a Dhéithe anois.
Is neartaítear sibh anois,
agus is athbheoitear na saolta uile.

Mar a bhí
Mar atá
Mar a bheas.

An Doirteadh ~ The Pouring-out

Placing the right hand over or upon the offering, the celebrant prays:

O Gods,
in accord with the tradition of our Ancestors, we offer you this
sacrifice.
May you bless
May you accept
May you consume
this chosen offering.

*The offering is poured out into the fire or onto the earth. A small
amount should remain in the offering bowl for the blessing—if
occurring—and for the éiric. Meanwhile the following is declared:*

As is given, so is taken,
and given back to you.

*After all offerings have been poured out save for a small amount for
subsequent blessings and the* éiric, *the celebrant continues:*

May the life of this offering grant you life, O Mighty Gods,
may it strengthen you and magnify you.

May all the worlds be blessed by the holiness of this offering,
and may it strengthen our Ancestors and our Beloved Dead,
especially (*list names of particular beloved dead*).
May you grant joy and tranquility to them, till we see them
again and join in their delight.

Now are you blessed, O Gods.
Now are you strengthened,
and all the worlds re-enlivened.

As it was
As it is
As it shall be.

Fáidheoireacht is Fleá ~ Divination and Feast

If a meditation, feast, divination, or other work is to be done, it is done now. The fire should remain lit, and the offering bowl remain on the altar undisturbed. The celebrant should wash their hands in lustral water before partaking in anything else, and then again before resuming the rite.

Naomhú ~ Blessing

The celebrant raises the offering bowl from the altar and, using an evergreen sprig or other suitable branch, circles the person, people, animal(s), or thing(s) to be blessed clockwise, sprinkling them with each line:

Neart fiaigh duibh daoibh (duit)
Neart iolair daoibh (duit)
Neart dreoilín

Neart toirní daoibh (duit)
Neart gealaí daoibh (duit)
Neart gréine

Neart talún daoibh (duit)
Neart mara daoibh (duit)
Neart neimhe

Altú agus Éiric ~ Thanksgiving and Reparation

The celebrant stands before the altar with hands raised and prays:

Gabhaimid buíochas libh, a Dhéithe Dhilse,
faoi gach aon sobharthan a thugadh.

Fáidheoireacht is Fleá ~ Divination and Feast

If a meditation, feast, divination, or other work is to be done, it is done now. The fire should remain lit, and the offering bowl remain on the altar undisturbed. The celebrant should wash their hands in lustral water before partaking in anything else, and then again before resuming the rite.

Naomhú ~ Blessing

The celebrant raises the offering bowl from the altar and, using an evergreen sprig or other suitable branch, circles the person, people, animal(s), or thing(s) to be blessed clockwise, sprinkling them with each line:

The strength of the raven be with you
The strength of the eagle be with you
The strength of the wren

The strength of the thunder be with you
The strength of the moon be with you
The strength of the sun

The strength of the earth be with you
The strength of the sea be with you
The strength of the sky

Altú agus Éiric ~ Thanksgiving and Reparation

The celebrant stands before the altar with hands raised and prays:

We give you thanks, O Dearest Gods,
for every blessing given.

The celebrant then says the following while pouring out the remaining offering into the fire or upon the earth. This éiric, that is "reparation", is made as a sign of our good will and best intentions in case some aspect or manner of our offering was displeasing to the Gods, the Ancestors, or the Land.

Má mí-labhair mé aon briathar,
Má mí-rinne mé aon gníomh,
Má mí-smaoinigh mé aon smaoineamh,
go nglaca sibh an íobairt seo
mar chomhartha dea-aigne is síochána
in éiric mo mhíghníomhartha.

An Scaradh ~ The Parting

With hands raised towards the people, or if solitary then to the altar, the celebrant says:

A Dhéithe Chumhachtacha,
Altaímid agus achainímid oraibh,
Beannaigí sinn,
ár dteaghlaigh,
gcairde is muintir,
Neartaigí sinn inár gcathanna,
Cuirigí fás fúinn le rath, sláinte, is eagna
le cóir na saolta.

Mar a bhí
Mar atá
Mar a bheas.

The rite is finished.

The celebrant then says the following while pouring out the remaining offering into the fire or upon the earth. This éiric, that is "reparation", is made as a sign of our good will and best intentions in case some aspect or manner of our offering was displeasing to the Gods, the Ancestors, or the Land.

If I have ill-spoken any word,
If I have ill-performed any deed,
If I have ill-thought any thought,
may you accept this offering
as a token of good-will and peace
in reparation for my misdeeds.

An Scaradh ~ The Parting

With hands raised towards the people, or if solitary then to the altar, the celebrant says:

O Mighty Gods,
We thank you and we entreat you,
Bless us,
our families,
friends and people,
Strengthen us in our trials,
Make us to grow in prosperity, health, and wisdom
for the right order of the worlds.

As it was
As it is
As it shall be.

The rite is finished.

3

Naomhú na n-Uiscí Naofa
Consecration of Lustral Water

One of the most frequently used aids to worship in our rituals is lustral water. The word "lustral" comes from the Latin lustrum (itself simply from the verb *luo* "I wash with water"). The lustrum is water used for purification, and in the Roman religion it is used in a ceremony every five years called the lustratio. In the Irish language it is simply referred to here as uisce naofa, literally "holy water".

Such a term and, indeed, the very use of holy water, may bring to mind parallels with the similar sacramental used in various Christian sects, particularly the Roman Catholic and Eastern Orthodox. Let us appreciate that this is in fact another attestation of how Europe did not convert to Christianity, rather Christianity converted to Europe. We find historically that the use of holy water, that is, blessed water that itself is able to confer blessing and cleansing to whomever and whatever it touches, is extraordinarily foreign to the Jewish religion, and by extension to Christianity in its original flourish. In Judaism, water is used ritually for ceremonial bathing to cleanse certain forms of ritual pollution in what is called a mikvah. The waters of the mikvah, however, do not possess any kind of blessing or special potency themselves. Similarly, ancient Christianity carried on this concept and extended it to the waters of baptism. Baptismal water was used singularly to symbolize by immersion the death of the former self tainted by original sin and the rising therefrom as a new, adopted child of God through the Christ. Again, the baptismal waters themselves possessed no blessing or inherent qualities.

It is among the European cultures (and several other polytheistic and animistic societies) that certain waters are seen to possess special sacred qualities *in themselves*. As in many indigenous cultures, the Irish recognize the numinous power in certain waters. The waters of the Well of Seaghais with its powers to confer wisdom, the life-giving waters of the River Boyne, or the healing waters of Tobar Sláine overseen by Dian Cécht. European Christianity, being as it is a syncretism of a Jewish-based Messianic cult and indigenous European religion, co-opted an immense amount of the practices and observances of the native religions, and among these was the use of holy water. Uisce naofa is ideally collected from a natural source such as a spring or collected rainwater. In the case of such waters, a ritual of blessing may not be necessary, especially if one has used the water before and developed a relationship with the land from where the waters come. For unknown waters or water from the tap or bought in a store, it is recommended to use the following blessing ritual. Water is like a conduit. It flows from one place to the next, carrying with it the characteristics and energies of where it's been. Just as water flowing past certain mineral deposits may take on a certain color, or water passing by a sewage plant becomes foul and unfit to drink unless properly filtered, so too do we ritually "filter" the collected water of any spiritual contamination it may have picked up, so that it may be suitable for ritual use.

The Rite Explained

The rite begins with a declaration of intention. The proper deities are then invoked, followed by the blessing of the waters itself. The waters are then proclaimed to be blessed, the deities are thanked, and the rite is ended. Ideally the rite should be followed by a deasghnáth an neimhidh to give offering to those same deities out of thanksgiving, either immediately afterwards or as soon as possible. The deities invoked are Manannán mac Lir, an Dagda, Aongus, Sionann and Bóinn.

Manannán is invoked, obviously, as lord of the seas and guardian of the waters. Sionann is invoked as she is the goddess and embodiment of the River Shannon. Similarly, Bóinn is the goddess of the River Boyne—she is the River Boyne.

An Dagda, Bóinn and Aongus are invoked in accord with the deep lore involving these three together. Though wife of Nechtan, she greatly desired an Dagda, who showed favor to her advances. This was no easy triste, as both had spouses who were not keen on sharing husband or wife's affections with others. The two met and had sex at Brú na Bóinne, i.e. Newgrange, on the winter solstice. A child was conceived. To conceal their affair from their spouses, an Dagda causes the sun to stand still until the child is born, and thus Aongus is born in a day. Therefore, by invoking these particular three, not only do we directly call upon that great goddess of the blessed River Boyne herself, but also our great father among the gods, and ask that the same desire which brought them together also be manifest in these lustral waters as well. Aongus himself is, in this sense, the very fulfillment of those desires, and to whom who is called Mac Óg (the young son, or, son of youth) belongs the deepest of our youthful desires, of abundance and joyful fecundity.

With each invocation, the basin holding the waters being blessed is held aloft towards a different direction. This ritual gesture isn't necessary if the basin is too large or if there's a concern the water may spill.

When invoking Manannán mac Lir, we hold the basin in the direction of the Atlantic Ocean. In Ireland this is going to be towards the west, for those in North America, to the east, etc. The reason is associated with our lore of Manannán being lord of Mag Mell, of the Land of Promise over the sea from Ireland. Those living on a large body of water may find more depth of meaning holding the basin for this first invocation towards that feature rather than the Atlantic. If in doubt, the best recourse is to divination.

The subsequent invocations to Sionann and Bóinn are made to the west and to the east respectively. This reflects the geographic locations of their rivers if one were standing in the center of Ireland. The fourth invocation also faces east for an Dagda in addition to the symbolism of the east as the place from which the sun rises. Eastward we face as we ask for blessings of increase, warmth and sanctity—attributes strongly associated with the heat of the rising sun and the promise a new day brings.

After the invocations come the ritual gestures of the blessing itself. It is proper and a powerful exercise to strongly visualize the four deities above and around you and imparting their blessing as the words are spoken. Take your time.

We spit into the water—a very ancient practice of healing and blessing rites in many indigenous cultures, ours included. Here we have a sacred joining of our own spittle, our own waters, with that which is provided by the Land Spirits and the Gods. *If there is a health or sanitary concern, this step may and should be skipped.*

We then thrust the fore and middle-fingers into the water in a symbolic union of celebrant with the spirit of the waters, a visceral visual echo of an Dagda's sexual union with Bóinn which brought forth youthful blessing and abundance, that is, Aongus himself. While declaring the new ninefold blessed nature of the waters, we stir the inserted fingers clockwise nine times with each declaration, "Waters of blessing (stir)...waters of protection (stir), etc".

After this, the ritual is completed with a series of thanks given to the deities invoked. Ideally the rite is followed immediately with a *deasghnáth an neimhidh* offered to those same deities as a proper thanksgiving.

Uses for Lustral Water

There are many uses for the water blessed in this rite. As already seen, the water is used in the main *deasghnáth an neimhidh*. Its use there exemplifies its main properties. As we declare in the rite for blessing the water, they have now taken on the following ninefold qualities: "...waters of blessing, waters of protection, waters of prosperity, waters of healing, waters of refuge, waters of strength, waters of peace, waters of friendship, waters of love." And so, the lustral water is now empowered to confer those same qualities upon the persons, places and things which they touch.

The three primary functions are **consecration**, **cleansing** and **protection**:

Consecration (Irish *naomhú*) The lustral waters can be used to consecrate, that is "make holy", what they touch. To make something holy is to set it aside as special in a particular way for the Gods and/or for ritual use. Some places, people and things have an innate holiness, such as a grove in the middle of an untouched forest, a scene of pure flowing waterfalls, the plateaus and sands of the desert under a starry sky, an innocent newborn baby, or the old sage made wise by years of experience, spiritual practice, and reflection. For other things, lustral water can be used to confer the qualities of holiness where they may not have been present before: a table once used as a nightstand now become an altar, a backyard usually used for social gatherings and barbecues temporarily consecrated to act as a sacred grove, or a bowl previously used for food now turned into an offering bowl. Obviously, it is not necessary to consecrate everything, nor would it be recommended. It is important to find a healthy balance in one's spiritual life, and allow for time, space, and objects to retain their simple, non-sacred use. Additionally, objects and spaces that have been consecrated ought to be set aside and respected thenceforth as holy and unfit for everyday use. To do otherwise effectively nullifies any consecration, and demonstrates a lack of care and awareness before the Gods.

Cleansing (Irish *ionnladh*) These waters are also used for cleansing, both in the physical and spiritual sense. As covered above, there is the natural need we have for using water to clean ourselves of dirt and any filth for our own refreshment as well as health. This extends to the symbolic use of water to affect a spiritual washing of our minds and souls of any mental distress. Thus, there are numerous instances in ritual where we may pour lustral water over our hands; in one instance for physically cleaning off the remnants of an offering that may have spilled slightly or stuck to the hands and doing so with a blessed substance to show the Gods our respect for this action, and in another instance the same gesture may be done to symbolically wash away the cares of the day so we can better focus on the sacred undertaking before us.

Protection (Irish *cosaint*) Importantly, the lustral water may be used to bestow the Gods' protection upon a person, place or thing. This features prominently in the primary *deasghnáth an neimhidh* as well as the house blessing and exorcism rites. In addition to these ceremonies, lustral water may sprinkled at any time when one feels the need to call down the protection of the Gods upon a place, or when asking for the Gods' blessing upon another or oneself.

Ritual Objects

The ritual objects for the *deasghnáth an neimhidh*. Since it is proper to follow the blessing of lustral water with a deasghnáth offering to the Gods and Goddesses invoked for the blessing, these objects and proper offerings should be ready and prepared. In addition:

Water basin – A basin suitable for holding water, large enough to hold the water without danger of spilling, but ideally small enough to be easily held aloft at the specified points of the ritual. The water to be blessed should be already in the basin prior to the start of the rite.

Naomhú na n-Uiscí Naofa ~ Consecration of Lustral Water

Fógairt ~ Declaration

Gairim ar na mara teacht i gcúnamh orm.
Naomhóidh mé
mar a naomhaíodh mo Shinsir
talamh go muir
muir go neamh
neamh go fearthainn
fearthainn go srúill
srúill go habhainn
abhainn go loch
loch go béal
béal go fuil
fuil go beatha.

Achainí ar Mhanannán ~ Invocation of Manannán

(*taking basin of water, collected from rain, stream, river, lake or sea, holding it aloft towards the Atlantic Ocean*)

A Mhanannáin! A Oirbsiu! A Mhac Lir!
Naomhaitheoir agus Suathaire na n-uiscí, go n-osclaí tú na geataí
idir an saol seo agus an saol eile
idir na huiscí os cionn agus na huiscí thíos
idir na huiscí seo agus na huiscí na mara.
Go ndealraí do sheacht mbeannacht ar na huiscí seo.
Go gcuire na huiscí seo rath mar na huiscí shaibhre do fhlaithis.
Go gcosnaí na huiscí seo mar a chosnaíonn an mhuir mhór Banbha bhreá.

Naomhú na n-Uiscí Naofa ~ Consecration of Lustral Water

Fógairt ~ Declaration

I call upon the seas to come to my aid.
I shall bless
as my Ancestors did bless
earth to sea
sea to sky
sky to rain
rain to stream
stream to river
river to lake
lake to mouth
mouth to blood
blood to life.

Achainí ar Mhanannán ~ Invocation of Manannán

(*taking basin of water, collected from rain, stream, river, lake or sea, holding it aloft towards the Atlantic Ocean*)

Manannán! Oirbsiu! Mac Lir!
Sanctifier and Stirrer of Waters, may you open the gates
between this world and the otherworld
between the waters above and the waters below
between these waters and the waters of the sea.
May your seven good blessings shine forth upon these waters.
May these waters bring prosperity like the rich waters of your kingdom
May these waters protect like the strong sea defends fair Banbha.

Achainí ar Shionainn ~ Invocation of Shannon
(holding basin towards the West)

A Shionainn! A Ghariníon Lir! A Bhandia na hAbhann!

A Thóraí na hEagna as Tobar Chonnla, a íobair tú tusa mar sladphraghas na heagna sin.

Gura na huiscí seo uiscí eagna mar na huiscí an Tobair Chonnla.

"Tobar Chonnla, ba mhór muirn,
ba faoin aibhéis eochair-ghorm:
sé srutha, narbh ionann bladh,
aiste, Sionainn an seachtú.

Naoi coill Chrimaill, an fhir ghlic,
cuireann thall faoin thobar dó:
atá le doilfe smachta
faoi cheo dorcha draíochta."

Go dtuga na huiscí seo eagna do na háiteanna a dtadhlaíonn siad, mar an Bhradán Eagna a shnámh sna n-uiscí an Tobair Chonnla.

Go dtuga na huiscí seo eagna do na daoine a dtadhlaíonn siad, mar Fhionn Mac Cumhaill a ith an Bhradán Eagna a shnámh sna n-uiscí an Tobair Chonnla.

Achainí ar Shionainn ~ Invocation of Shannon
(holding basin towards the West)

Shannon (Sionainn)! Granddaughter of Lir! Goddess of the River!

O Seeker of wisdom from Connla's Well, you gave yourself for the price of that wisdom.

May these waters be waters of wisdom like the waters of the Well of Connla.

"Connla's Well, great its sound,
was beneath the reef-blue abyss:
six streams, without equal in fame,
rise up from it, Shannon being the seventh.

Nine hazelnuts of Crimall the cunning man,
drop their fruits there beneath the well:
standing by mystic power
under a dark mist of druidry."[4]

May these waters bring wisdom to the places they touch, like the Salmon of Wisdom who swam in the waters of Connla's Well.

May these waters bring wisdom to the people they touch, like Fionn mac Cumhaill who ate the Salmon of Wisdom who swam in the waters of Connla's Well.

Achainí ar Bhóinn ~ Invocation of Boann (Boyne)
(holding basin towards the East)

A Bhóinn! A Sheaghais! A Eithne!
Bóinn, a dtug an Daghda an ghrian chun socair le naoi mí ar a
son go dtí an bhreith an Aongus Díograise.
Bóinn, a raibh a haon guí leis an Daghda a aontaigh.
Bóinn, a thothlaigh an eagna an Tobair Seaghaise, agus a bhuail
a uiscí í.
Go mbronna na huiscí seo áilleacht ar na háiteanna, daoine, agus
rudaí a thadhlaíonn siad, mar a tuismigh tú Aongus is Áille.
Go réala na huiscí seo na dea-dhúile croíthe na ndaoine a
thadhlaíonn siad.

Nár bhá na huiscí seo sinn mar an Tobar Seaghais:

"Nechtain mac Labrada lonn,
dár bhean Bóinn, dearbhaím,
tobar diamhair ba 'na dhún,
asat mhaidhm gach mí-rún.
Níl aon le fáil a dhearcfadh ar a lár
nach madhmfadh a dhá rosc rinn:
dá ngluaisfeadh sé ar clé nó deis,
ní thiocfadh sé uaidh gan aithis"

ach ina áit sin, gura na huiscí seo an tobar a bhuinníonn gach
uile maitheas,
a thugann naofacht do na súile, slánú don chorp, suaimhneas
don mheabhair, cairdeas idir cairde, agus grá idir gach uile dea-
dhaoine.

Achainí ar Bhóinn ~ Invocation of Boann (Boyne)
(holding basin towards the East)

Boann! Segais! Eithne!
Boann, for whom the Daghda made the sun stand still for nine
months until the birth of fair Aongus the Beloved.
Boann, whose one wish was to unite with the Daghda.
Boann, who craved the wisdom of the Well of Segais, and whose
waters overcame her.
May these waters bestow beauty on the places, people, and
things they touch, as you brought forth Aongus the Fair.
May these waters manifest the good-desires of the hearts of the
people they touch.

May these waters not drown us as the Well of Segais:

"Nechtain son of Labraid the fierce,
whose wife was Boann, I affirm;
a secret well there was in his haven,
from which surged every ill-rune.
There was none that would look to its bottom
but his two bright eyes would burst:
if he should move to left or right,
he would not come from it without reproach"[5]

but rather may these waters be a well
which gushes forth every kind of good, which brings blessing
to the eyes, healing to the body, peace to the mind, friendship
between friends, and love between all good people.

Achainí ar an Dagda agus Naofú ~ Invocation of the Dagda and Consecration

(holding basin in center, facing East)

A Dhagda!
A Eochaid Ollathair!
A Ruadh Ro-Fessa!

A líon Bóinn bhreá le do shíol le searc agus grá uirthi,
Go naomhaí tú *(spit into water)*,
Go dtreá tú *(insert fore- and middle-finger into water)*, agus
Go líona tú na huiscí seo *(stir waters clockwise)* le do naofacht,
ionas go dtuismí siad an dea-dhúil an chroí, chun go mbeidís
uiscí beannachta
uiscí cosanta
uiscí ratha
uiscí leighis
uiscí tearmainn
uiscí urra
uiscí síochána
uisci cairdis
uiscí grá

Is beannaithe na huiscí seo anois.

Is áit bheannaithe í an áit a gcroitheann iad.
Is rud beannaithe é an rud a bhfaigheann iad.
Is duine beannaithe é an duine a bhfaigheann iad.

Buíochas le Manannán a thugann bheannacht na Mara Móire.
Buíochas leis an Dagda a bhronann a shearc agus a chumhacht
ar na huiscí.
Buíochas le hAongus a tháinig amach as an grá na habhann-
uiscí.

Buíochas le Sionann a thug féin mar íobairt ar son na heagna.
Buíochas le Bóinn a thóraigh agus a shroich an dea-dhúil a croí.

Buíochas lena Dea-Dhúile Chaomhnaithe na tíre seo as na huiscí mhaithe a riarann siad.
Buíochas le mo Shinsir as an bheatha an choirp agus na nósanna a tháinig siad anuas chugam.
Buíochas le na Déithe as gach uile maith.

Mar a bhí
Mar atá
Mar a bheas.

(*The rite is finished*)

Achainí ar an Dagda agus Naofú ~ Invocation of the Dagda and Consecration

(holding basin in center, facing East)

A Dhagda!
A Eochaid Ollathair!
A Ruadh Ro-Fessa!

Who filled fair Bóinn with your seed in love and good-desire,
May you bless (*spit into water*),
penetrate (*insert forefinger and middle finger into water*),
and fill these waters (*stir waters clockwise*) with your good-blessing,
that they too may bring forth the good-desire of the heart, to be
waters of blessing
waters of protection
waters of prosperity
waters of healing
waters of refuge
waters of strength
waters of peace
waters of friendship
waters of love

These waters are now blessed.

The place where they are sprinkled is a blessed place.
The thing which receives them is a blessed thing.
The person who receives them is a blessed person.

Thanks be to Manannán who gives the blessing of the Great Sea.
Thanks be to the Dagda who grants his love and power to the waters.
Thanks be to Aongus who came forth from the love of the river waters.

Thanks be to Sionann who gave herself for wisdom.

Thanks be to Bóinn who sought and attained the good-desire of her heart.

Thanks be to the good Guardian Spirits of this land for the good waters they provide.

Thanks be to my Ancestors for the life of the body and ways they have given me.

Thanks be to the Gods for all.

As it was

As it is

As it ever shall be.

(*The rite is finished*)

(*An offering, starting with the* Ullmhú Íobartha *may follow, offered to Manannán, an Dagda, Aongus, Sionann, and Bóinn.*)

4

Beannú Tí
House Blessing

There is no place more necessarily guarded and protected than the home. It's the place where we spend so much of our lives, where some of us raise our families, create, work, eat and sleep. Having elaborated on some of the principal meanings of blessing and consecration in the previous rites, we have a solid understanding for why this is important and what this ritual action may accomplish. This blessing will ward the home and consecrate it to be a place of good fortune and particular protection, without the intention of rendering it for ritual use, but with the understanding that it is a place guarded and favored by the Gods, being the home of people or a person who honors them, the Ancestors and the Land.

The Rite Explained

Before beginning this rite, it is ideal to set the house in proper order. Our ancestral folklore, as well as that of neighboring traditions, emphasizes with peculiar specificity and repetition just how important a clean, well-ordered home is to the numinous beings around us. This is particularly important to the Land spirits, and sensibly so as we walk their ground and drink their water peaceably only at their good favor. Therefore, they are keen to notice and take offense at the disrespect of a tenant on their territory who treats it—and therefore, them— carelessly and dishonorably. Additionally, we see in surviving lore certain deities themselves who oversee the proper order of the home. In our own tradition, we see this prominently with Brigid and perhaps, to an extent, with the Morrígan as powerful queen of sovereignty whose provenance is the right order of her land and people.

Having cleaned up and set the house in order, the celebrant prepares a basin of lustral water for sprinkling. The sprinkling may be done by dipping and flicking the fingers, or additionally elevated by using a sprig of evergreen, a use attested and revived in the Norse & Germanic traditions. The celebrant also has a candle or lamp prepared which will be lit during the ceremony. The candle or lamp should be of a sort that is easily held and carried throughout the house. A taper with a wind guard for the flame, for example. Finally, just as in the rite for blessing lustral water, it is proper to follow this ritual with an offering to the deities invoked therein, and so those offerings should be prepared and ready beforehand.

The basin of lustral water is set outside the front door of the house along with the unlit lamp. If this is not practical, the rite may begin in the center of the main room of the home. Facing the main doorway of the house, we sprinkle lustral water towards the doorway, then above and below. After this, we circle the house clockwise three times while sprinkling lustral water. This is an act of blessing to the Land spirits of the property.

After this, the fire is lit upon the candle or lamp. This action invokes the assistance and presence of the Ancestors to the rite. We then proceed straight to calling upon four particular deities: Manannán mac Lir, Brigid, an Morrígan and Lugh. Manannán is invoked first, as he casts the *féth fíada*, the mist of invisibility, between this world and the other. Brigid is called upon not only for her care over so many aspects of the hearth and domestic life, but importantly for her power as protectress, as she whose mantle blesses and protects, and whose flame illuminates the darkness, casting out all that is harmful and unwell. Next, we invoke the Morrígan. As explained above, this is out of her great power and care for the land and people, the sovereignty of which is her embodiment and realm. Indeed, her fierce qualities might be compared to that of the mother bear—nurturing and caring to her own and ensuring their protection and abundance, while being ferociously protective, destructive and terrifying to those who threaten or dishonor what is hers. Finally, we invoke Lugh, shining king among the Gods. Not only do we turn to him for his immense power to fight off all that is malignant and malicious from our lives and homes, but especially for his defending fatherly guardianship which we see so poignantly in his defense of Cú Chulainn when the latter, severely wounded and exhausted, was at last granted some respite warded by the divine Lugh who fought off his enemies until he was rested and able to return to battle.

Having called upon these powerful divinities, we begin the blessing of the interior of the home. The door to the home is opened and, standing before the threshold, the celebrant asks the Gods to be present therein, and then proceeds to sprinkle towards the inside of the home three times in blessing. We then proceed throughout the rooms of the house, preferably in clockwise manner, bearing the lighted flame and sprinkling lustral water in each room while saying the blessing prayer.

Having gone through each room, we return to the main door and, this time facing out, once again sprinkle here thrice, followed by the same action one more time towards the inside. After this, the home is declared blessed. Ideally a *deasghnáth an neimhidh* then follows, with offerings made to Manannán mac Lir, Brigid, an Morrígan and Lugh.

Ritual Objects

Water basin – A basin or bowl holding lustral water. This should be small enough to carry comfortably throughout the house.

Candle or **Lamp** – A sort of candle or lamp that is easily lit and carried throughout the house without risk of being dropped or having the flame easily put out.

Evergreen sprig – An optional addition to the ceremony, this may be used to dip into and sprinkle the lustral water.

Offerings for the *deasghnáth an neimhidh* – Offerings suitable to be offered to Manannán mac Lir, Brigid, an Morrígan and Lugh after the blessing is complete.

Beannú Tí ~ House Blessing

Croitheadh uisce naofa ~ Sprinkling of lustral water

*The celebrant takes the lustral water and stands outside the house
before the front door. If unable to be outside, stand in the central part
of the home.*

Gairim ar Talamh, ar Muir is ar Neamh, teacht i gcúnamh orainn.
*(sprinkles water towards the doorway of home or center of house three
times: towards the base, the center, then above)*

Sprinkling towards each direction named:

Thoir bláth
Theas séis
Thiar fios
Thuaidh cath
In idirmheán flaith

*Sprinkling around the outside of the house clockwise insofar as able,
saying:*

Go naomhaítear duit, a Theach is a Thalaimh,
an áit a gcónaíonn na Dea-Dhúile na Tíre seo.
Go naomhaítear daoibh, go naomhaítear daoibh,
go naomhaítear daoibh, agus go raibh dea-aigne eadrainn.

Lasadh na tine ~ Lighting of the fire

The celebrant or other participant lights the fire.

Tógaim an tine seo
i láthair na Dea-Dhúl na Tíre seo,
i láthair na Sinsear
i láthair na nDéithe

gan fiarán, gan danartha, gan díomas,
agus i measc na dTrí Neimheadh dár dtearmann.

Beannú Tí ~ House Blessing

Croitheadh uisce naofa ~ Sprinkling of lustral water

The celebrant takes the lustral water and stands outside the house before the front door. If unable to be outside, stand in the central part of the home.

I call upon Earth, upon Sea and Sky, to come to our aid. (*sprinkles water towards the doorway of home or center of house three times: towards the base, the center, then above*)

Sprinkling towards each direction named:

Prosperity in the east
Music in the south
Knowledge in the west
Battle in the north
Sovereignty in the center

Sprinkling around the outside of the house clockwise insofar as able, saying:

May you be blessed, O House and Soil,
the place where dwell the Good Spirits of this Land.
May you be blessed, may you be blessed,
may you be blessed, and may there be good-will between us.

Lasadh na tine ~ Lighting of the fire

The celebrant or other participant lights the fire.

I kindle this fire
in the presence of the good spirits of this land
in the presence of the Ancestors
in the presence of the Gods

without petulance, without cruelty, without arrogance,
and amid the Three Holies for our refuge.

Achainí ar na Déithe ~ Invocation of the Gods

Manannán mac Lir

A Mhanannáin
A Oirbsiu
A Mhac Lir

A thiarnaíonn do na mara móra
Agus a osclaíonn na geataí idir an saol seo agus an saol eile,
Oscail na geataí, agus bí linn sa tigh seo.

An Morrígan

A Mhorrigan
A Mhacha
A Bhadb

A fhaigheann bua thar ár naimhde
Tar agus cuidigh linn i gach cathú dá bhfuilimid ann,
agus bí linn sa teach seo.

Bríd

A Bhríd
A Ní-Dhagda
A Tine Tinfidh

Leath orainn do bhrat,
Tú lasair an-mhór na heagna sa dorchadas.
Bí linn sa teach seo.

Lugh

A Lugh
A Lámhfhada
A Ildánach

Cosain sinn agus cuir cath as ár n-ucht,
mar a throid tú as ucht na nDéithe agus a sheachain tú do
mhacsa ina scís.
Bí linn sa tigh seo.

Achaní ar na Déithe ~ Invocation of the Gods

Manannán mac Lir

A Mhanannáin
A Oirbsiu
A Mhac Lir

Who rules over the great seas
And who opens the gates between this world and the Otherworld
We beseech you, open the gates! And be with us in this house.

An Morrígan

A Mhorrigan
A Mhacha
A Bhadb

Who grants victory over our enemies:
Come and aid us in every struggle we are in,
and be with us in this house.

Bríd

A Bhríd
A Ní-Dhagda
A Tine Tinfidh

Spread your mantle over us,
You, great fire of wisdom in the darkness.
Be with us in this house.

Lugh

A Lugh
A Lámhfhada
A Ildánach

Guard us and do battle for us,
as you fought on behalf of the Gods and shielded your son in
his weariness.
Be with us in this house.

Beannú tí ~ House blessing

Open main door of the home and, at the threshold of the house, say:

Déithe sa teach! Déithe sa teach! Déithe sa teach!

Standing at the threshold facing into the house, raise hands-or at least right hand-and say:

Go mbeannaí na Déithe an teach seo ó bhonn go ceann,

Sprinkle the door from top, then middle, then threshold with lustral water, saying:

go mbeannaí siad an t-aer, an t-uisce, an talamh,

Now move throughout the rooms of the house with the lighted flame, sprinkling with lustral water once in the middle of the room, and once towards each door and window, while saying the following verses:

Go mbeannaí siad an bord agus a bhia,
gach leaba agus a duine.

Go leatha an doras don deoraí go fial
go dté an cara sa teach seo i ngaol,
go raibh seisean an dún in aghaidh na cora an tsaoil.

Returning now to the main door of the house, say:

Go líontar an teach seo le tuiscint, le comhtheacht is carthanacht.

Sprinkle the main door of the home from lintel, then middle, then threshhold, saying:

Go gcosnaí na Déithe an teaghlach seo ar gach aon braodar, fala is baol.

Sprinkle three times towards inside of the home, saying:

Agus go gcuire na Déithe an rath oraibh, anois, anocht is i gcónaí.

The blessing is now complete.

Beannú tí ~ House blessing

Open main door of the home and, at the threshold of the house, say:

The Gods be in this house! The Gods be in this house! The Gods be in this house!

Standing at the threshold facing into the house, raise hands-or at least right hand-and say:

May the Gods bless this house from bottom to top,

Sprinkle the door from top, then middle, then threshold with lustral water, saying:

may they bless the air, the water, ground,

Now move throughout the rooms of the house with the lighted flame, sprinkling with lustral water once in the middle of the room, and once towards each door and window, while saying the following verses:

May they bless the table and its food,
every bed and its person.

May the door open wide with hospitality for the stranger,
may the friend come to be family in this house,
may it be a refuge in the face of the twists and turns of life.

Returning now to the main door of the house, say:

May this house be filled with understanding, harmony and friendship,

Sprinkle the main door of the home from lintel, then middle, then threshhold, saying:

May the Gods guard this family against every worry, resentment and danger.

Sprinkle three times towards inside of the home, saying:

And may the Gods prosper you, now, tonight and always.

The blessing is now complete.

Is áit bheannaithe í an áit seo anois.

Buíochas lena Dea-Dhúile Chaomhnaithe na Tíre seo: coimeádaigí an áit seo agus na daoine uile a bhfuil ina gcónaí anseo.
Buíochas le mo Shinsir, a sheachnaíonn a síol ar anachain uile.
Buíochas leis an Morrigan, Bríd, is Lugh, as gach uile maith, a chosnaíonn an áit seo is gach duine inti, agus a naomhaíonn í as a dtobar uile mhaitheasa.

As it was
As it is
As it shall be.

The place is now blessed, the rite is finished.

This place is now a blessed place.

Thanks be to the good spirts of this land: protect this place and all the people who make their dwelling here.
Thanks be to my Ancestors, who shield their descendant from all calamity.
Thanks be to the Morrigan, Brigid, and Lugh, for every good, who protect this place and every person in it, and who hallow it from their font of all goodness.

As it was
As it is
As it shall be.

The place is now blessed, the rite is finished.

5

The Festivals

From ancestral times we have observed the regular rhythmic cycles of the sun, moon, stars and natural world around us. The celestial place of sun and moon gave rise to our calendars, and served as a guide to the ebbs and flows of nature—the coming of spring, the coming of summer, the proper time to begin harvest, the warning of frosts to come. It is these latter occasions tied to the growth and harvest cycle which our Ancestors handed down to us as festivals of the highest magnitude, the Fire Festivals, *na Féilte Tine*.

The Fire Festivals

The Fire Festivals are the greatest ceremonial times of the year. Their observance is recorded in the most ancient surviving texts we have, and given their coinciding with the alignments of several megalithic monuments, passage tombs and burial mounds, we can know their celebration reaches far back into the ancestral past.

There are four fire festivals, which occur every three months:

> **Samhain** – from sunset on October 31 until sunset on November 1.
> **Imbolc** – from sunset on January 31 until sunset on February 1.
> **Bealtaine** – from sunset on April 30 until sunset on May 1.
> **Lughnasadh** – from sunset on July 31 until sunset on August 1.

The ancestral Irish and other Celtic peoples, much like other pre-modern populations, reckoned the period of a day as starting at sunset of what modern reckoning considers the day before.

Just as the day is seen as consisting of two halves, beginning with the dark half of night and concluding with the brightness of day, so also is the year split, starting with the dark half of winter preceding the light summer half. This bifurcation of the year into two great seasons rather than the modern, conventional four is typical of the Celtic worldview.

Samhain
Oct 31 – Nov 1

This is our new year festival and great day of honoring the ancestors and our beloved dead. Set precisely between the autumnal equinox and the winter solstice, this is the time in the northern hemisphere when the shift to winter is keenly felt, with the northerly reaches feeling their first frosts. In traditional Ireland it is the time to move from the summer pasture lands back to the sturdier homes and settlements to endure the winter. The harvest is ended, and the time to rely on meat becoming more necessary and thus a time of slaughter has come. The festival recurs again and again in our lore. It is on this great night that an Dagda and an Morrígan came together before the Battle of Magh Tuireadh. It was on this night (though elsewhere it may have been on the winter solstice) that Bóinn joined with an Dagda at Newgrange and, the Dagda causing the sun to stand still, Bóinn conceived and gave birth to Aongus.

Ever present in our folklore is the knowledge that on the night of October 31, *Oíche Shamhna* (Samhain Eve), we are on the threshold of this world and the Otherworld, and the inhabitants thereof are wont to pass into ours at this time. Some say that the souls of the departed from the past year enter into the Otherworld this night, and so this is the penultimate time to honor those who have passed on.

The Samhain Rite

It is fitting to wait until just before sunset to begin the ceremony for *Oíche Shamhna*. From ancient times all the hearth fires were put extinguished prior to Samhain Eve, so that they could be lit anew from the great fires lit on the hilltops this night. If one has such a hearth fire, it is of course proper to carry on this eldest of traditions. Regardless, those of us in a more common contemporary setting may replicate the solemnity of this occasion by turning off all electric lights, appliances, cellphones and other devices. Then the Samhain fire is lit in a deep, pregnant silence, giving birth to the new year.

The lighting of the fire itself is prefaced by a solemn declaration that the old year has ended, followed by a slow and somber procession nine times around the ceremonial space while giving thanks for the year gone by. In this rite the procession may be made counterclockwise, an act of significant gravity since at all other times we should move around the grove and sacred fire clockwise. This counterclockwise movement on this one singular occasion signifies many things: that contrary to the clockwise motion which mimics the sun and thus the rhythms of life, we are now manifesting the motions of death; that whereas at all other times we move clockwise as the right motion of this world, on this night we move in the opposite direction as those who dwell in the Otherworld. For some, counterclockwise movement is interpreted as a stirring of ill-favor regardless of the occasion, and so for those who observe that practice this procession may be performed clockwise. There is no need for undue discomfort, worry or scruples at this most holy time of year! Additionally, during these declarations, we pause and look to the west, also making our invocations in that direction rather than the typical east. This too signifies that we turn our gaze towards the west, toward the ancestral direction of death and what lies beyond, for even today we retain the tradition that the land of promise, the Otherworld, lies somewhere beyond the west. The fire is then lit, preferably from friction or flint, and the birth of the new year declared.

We then invoke Donn, the great ancestor of ancestors, one of the first among the sons of Mil. It is said that he was among those who led the first venture to Ireland, but was slain before he could reach the land itself. His burial mound is Bull Rock off the southwestern coast of Ireland, a precipitous and rocky mount in the sea known for ages as Teach Duinn, that is *the House of Donn*. For centuries our ancestors said of the dead that *they have gone to the House of Donn*. In our invocation we honor this greatest of grandfathers among our Ancestors, and ask him to open the way between the world of the dead and our own, that we may honor our beloved dead this night.

After this follows the invocations of an Dagda, Bóinn and Aongus. See the above rite of blessing for lustral water for more on the lore regarding these three and the significance of their relationship relating to Samhain. Other deities whom our Ancestors honored on *Oíche Shamhna*, the tradition of which we may do well to continue, include Mongfind the fair-haired and Tlachtga. After this the ceremony itself proceeds as in the typical *deasghnáth an neimhidh*. It is fitting to make a great occasion out of this night, with an atmosphere both somber and reflective at times, and at others joyous—even raucous—with games and festivities. If at all possible, it's the perfect time for divination, even if one does not usually have recourse to it.

Samhain

Croitheadh leis uisce naofa ~ Blessing with lustral water
As usual

Lasadh na tine Shamhna ~ Lighting of the Samhain fire
The kindling for a suitably large fire is prepared. Shortly before sunset, all lights are extinguished, all electronics are powered off and, if possible, unplugged. At sunset the celebrant declares, facing West:

Fuair an seanbhliain bás, agus tá an bhliain nua ar baraíd teacht.
Agus táimid anseo inár seasamh idir ann is as
idir inné is amárach
idir breith is bás
idir talamh, muir, is neamh
idir an saol seo, an saol eile, is an saol thíos.

Ón am gan thús, ón seanaithinne a d›adhain an cruinne, tógaimis
den Sheantine agus adhnaimis bliain úr.

*Celebrant and others stand in the West, facing center & then walk
nine times about the center, slowly saying each line. After every three
circles, stand in West for a moment of reflection and thanks:*

Faoin thalamh mhaith a chothaigh sinn...
Faoin fhearthainn mhaith a mhéadaigh sinn...
Faoin ghaoth bheatha a bheoigh sinn...
Gabhaimid buíochas leis an bhliain a chuaigh thart.

Faoina ghaolta a threisigh orainn...
Faoina chairde a neartaigh sinn...
Faoina Mhairbh Mhuirneacha a stiúir sinn igceart...
Gabhaimid buíochas leis an bhliain a chuaigh thart.

Faoin bhliain a maireamar inti...
Faoin chruinne a bhfoghlaimíomar inti...
Faoina Dhéithe agus a mbeannachtaí gan áireamh...
Gabhaimid buíochas les an bhliain a chuaigh thart.

Samhain

Croitheadh leis uisce naofa ~ Blessing with lustral water
As usual

Lasadh na tine Shamhna ~ Lighting of the Samhain fire
The kindling for a suitably large fire is prepared. Shortly before sunset, all lights are extinguished, all electronics are powered off and, if possible, unplugged. At sunset the celebrant declares, facing West:

The old year has died, and the new year about to arrive.
And here we stand between here and there
between yesterday and tomorrow
between birth and death
between earth, sea, and sky
between this world, the otherworld, and the underworld.

From the time without beginning, from the ancient spark which ignited the universe, let us take of the primordial fire and kindle a new year.

Celebrant and others stand in the West, facing center & then walk nine times about the center, slowly saying each line. After every three circles, stand in West for a moment of reflection and thanks:

For the good earth which sustained us...
For the good rain which helped us to grow...
For the living breath which vivified us...
We give thanks to the year gone by.

For the family who supported us...
For the friends who strengthened us...
For the Beloved Dead who guided us aright...
We give thanks to the year gone by.

For the year in which we lived...
For the universe in which we experienced...
For the Gods and their countless blessings...
We give thanks to the year gone by.

After reflection in the West, approach the kindling, standing in the West and center. Lighting the fire, say:

Lasaim an Úr Tine Seo

Trína Dhéithe, Trína Shinsir, Trína Dhea-Neacha na Tíre Seo
Ón Shaol Seo, Ón Shaol Eile, Ón Shaol Thíos
Den Thalamh, Den Mhuir, Den Neamh.

Tar amach, Úrbhliain! Tar amach! Tar amach!
(*as flame begins to quicken*) Rugadh Úrbhliain dúinn!

After reflection in the West, approach the kindling, standing in the West and center. Lighting the fire, say:

I light This New Fire

By the Gods, By the Ancestors, By the Good Spirits of this Land
From this World, From the Otherworld, From the Underworld
Of Earth, Of Sea, Of Sky

Come forth, New Year! Come forth! Come forth!
(*as flame begins to quicken*) A New Year is born to us!

Achainí ar Donn ~ Invocation of Donn

Celebrant or other lights a taper from the Samhain fire and holds it aloft facing the West:

A Dhuinn! An Donn, Dath na Talún!
A Dhuinn, an Dorcha, an Chéad Cheann den Chlann Mhíle!
An Chéad Sinsear, an Chéad Té a shiúlann is a ghiollaíonn na Hallaí Báis, Tusa a tháinig isteach sa Saol Eile trína n-uiscí an iardheiscirt chomh luath i ndiaidh a chonaic Tú Éire.

A Dhuinn, a Dhorcha, a Dhoinn, a Dhath na Talún!
An Té a chuireann fáilte romhainn go dtí an Oileán Thiar a bhfuil do Theach nuair a dhéanfaimid ár dturas ón shaol seo chun an tsaoil eile.

A Athair, a ndéanann a hallaí áit don iomlán na sochraidí mhochta, a ndéanamid sos i do Thigh i ndeireadh ár gcúrsa anseo.
Is tanaí é an brat idir na saolta ar an oíche seo, an oíche seo, ar an oíche is naofa is aduaine seo!
Oscail a Dhuinn a Dhorcha a Dhoinn, le do thoil, na geataí idir an saol seo, eile is thíos!

Tagaigí agus bígí linn, a Shinsir dhil gheal!
Fáilte romhaibh, fáilte romhaibh, agus fáilte is trí romhaibh, a Aithreacha is a Mháithreacha,
A Sheanaithreacha is a Sheanmháithreacha,
Le ríomh siar go tosach aimsire.
Beannaím daoibh, a ghaolta dhil
agus go mbeannaí sibh féin dúinn,
le bheith ag gardáil ár n-anama is ár gcoirp,
anois agus inár gcruachás.
Míle altú buí libh as bhur gcabhair is gcion,
agus míle fáilte romhaibh go dtí an neimheadh ar an oíche is naofa seo!

Achainí ar Donn ~ Invocation of Donn

*Celebrant or other lights a taper from the Samhain fire and holds it
aloft facing the West:*

Donn! The Brown, of Earthly Hue!
Donn, the Dark, the First of the Children of Mil!
The First Ancestor, first to walk and keep the Halls of Death,
who entered the Otherworld through the southwestern waters
after sighting Éire.

Donn, the Dark, the Brown, of Earthly Hue!
Who welcome us at the Western Isle where is Your House,
as we fare from this world to the next world.

Father, whose halls make room for all the mighty hosts, in
whose House we rest at the end of our journey here. The veil is
thin between the worlds on this night, this night, on this night
most holy and strange! O Donn, Dark and Brown, by your will,
open the gates between this World, the Other, and Under!

Come and be with us, O Dearly Beloved Ancestors!
You are welcome, you are welcome, you are thrice over welcome,
O Fathers and Mothers,
Grandfathers and Grandmothers,
Stretching back to the beginning of time.
We bless you, dearest kin
and may you bless us,
guarding our souls and our bodies,
now and in time of distress.
A thousand thanks to you for your assistance and love, and a
thousand welcomes to you to the grove on this holy night!

Achainí ar na Déithe ~ Invocation of the Gods
An Dagda

A Dhagda! A Eochaid Ollathair! A Ruadh Ro-Fessa!

A líon Bóinn bhreá le do shíol
le searc agus grá uirthi ar an oíche seo,
Go naomhaí tú linn agus bí linn anocht.

Bóinn

A Bhóinn! A Sheaghais! A Eithne!

Bóinn, a dtug an Daghda an ghrian chun socair le naoi mí
ar a son go dtí an bhreith an Aongus Díograise.
Bóinn, a raibh a haon guí leis an Daghda a aontaigh.
Go naomhaí tú linn agus bí linn anocht.

Aongus

A Aongus! A Mhac Óg! A Mhac Daghda

A rinne nithiúil an grá in aisling amharctha. Agus a chuireann i
gcrích fíor-dhúil an chroí. An Té a rugadh ar an oíche seo anocht!
Go naomhaí tú linn agus bí linn anocht.

Na Déithe uile ~ All the Gods

Gairim ar na Déithe Uile Ró-Naofa,
Na Déithe Buacha na Talún, Mara, is Neimhe,
Na Déithe ár Sinsear ó thosach aimsire.
Go naomhaí sibh linn agus bígí linn anocht.

The rest of the rite follows as the ordinary housel, save for the Blessing, the Naomhú na Shamhna, *which is done by having two individuals take two brands lit from the Samhain Fire. All present then walk between the brands while the celebrant proclaims over them* the Neart Fiaigh Duibh daoibh, *etc.*

The rite concludes as usual; however, the Samhain Fire is left to burn out of its own accord.

Achaini ar na Déithe ~ Invocation of the Gods
An Dagda

A Dhagda! A Eochaid Ollathair! A Ruadh Ro-Fessa!

Who did fill fair Bóinn with Your seed
in love and good-desire on this night,
May you bless us and be with us tonight.

Bóinn

Bóinn! Segais! Eithne!

Bóinn, for whom the Daghda made the sun stand still
for nine months until the birth of fair Aongus the Beloved.
Bóinn, whose one wish was to unite with the Daghda.
May you bless us and be with us tonight.

Aongus

A Aongus! A Mhac Óg! A Mhac Daghda

Who made real the love of your vision, and manifests the heart's
true love and desire,
Who was born on this night!
May you bless us and be with us tonight.

Na Déithe uile ~ All the Gods

I call upon all the Most-Holy Gods,
The Victorious Gods of Earth, Sea, and Sky,
The Gods of our Ancestors from the beginning of time,
May you bless us and be with us tonight.

The rest of the rite follows as the ordinary housel, save for the Blessing, the Naomhú na Shamhna, *which is done by having two individuals take two brands lit from the Samhain Fire. All present then walk between the brands while the celebrant proclaims over them* the Neart Fiaigh Duibh daoibh, *etc.*

The rite concludes as usual; however, the Samhain Fire is left to burn out of its own accord.

Imbolc
Jan 31 – Feb 1

The second of the great fire festivals occurs just as we pass from the deepest part of winter. In many parts of the northern hemisphere that experience a cold winter, it is about this time that the first rumblings of spring occur. Indeed, in some latitudes the very first wildflowers may begin to spring forth, while in others this may only be the first thaw in a much longer cold season. In any case, this is the time when the natural world begins to reawaken, and the rekindling of the fire of life beckons to us as well.

Most appropriately, from ancestral times this festival has been sacred to Brigid (Modern Irish spelling *Bríd*), and so nowadays it is most commonly called *Lá Fhéile Bríde*, the day of Brigid's festival. Brigid's very name is conjectured to mean *the Exalted One*. She is associated with fire, and is a triple-goddess, having dominion over the arts of poetry, healing and smith-work. Hers is the fire of the forge as smith, and she kindles the *fire in the head*, the fire of wise and poetic inspiration.

There is an abundance of lore surrounding this day. We see the recurring theme of Brigid coming to visit the homes of her devotees. Her followers gather on the evening of her feast day (that is, the evening of January 31st) for food and merriment, having collected fresh rushes. These rushes are fashioned into three- or four-armed patterns called Brigid's Crosses. These are assembled after dinner, with one custom being to lay the rushes allotted for each person on the table under their plate while eating. In the course of the evening, one girl or young woman is chosen to represent Brigid. She goes out of the house and a tradition reenacted from pre-written times is enacted in which she knocks on the door with a call-and-response with those within. As she enters, those inside kneel and hail Brigid's welcome, asking her blessing. At night, strips of cloth or whole garments may be hung outside for Brigid to bless as she passes through the world this night. These cloths or clothing may then be worn at any time of sickness in the year to come to invoke the great goddess' healing care. Another salutary custom is the preparation and procession of the *Brídeóg*, a crafted effigy of the goddess herself. This may take various forms, but is constructed with devotion to the Exalted One on the night of her festival, laid in a decorated bed overnight, and then processed through the town and surrounding lands during the following day, granting blessing and shooing away the cold of winter and cold of heart.

The Imbolc Rite

The celebration begins before the evening meal with the usual sprinkling of lustral water, following by the lighting of the sacred fire. This fire may be the more customary outdoor fire, but as this time of year is generally quite cold for most in the northern hemisphere, the rite assumes an indoor celebration. In that case, the fire lit may be in one's hearth, or in lieu of a hearth, a large candle or three branched candelabra (representing the triple nature of Brigid) may be prepared. Easily held candles are also prepared which will be blessed in the course of the rite and then distributed to those present. Taper lights work ideally for this, and may be collected in a basket of sort so they are in one place for the blessing and then handed off to each person.

The fire is lit and, once it is reliably aflame, blessed thrice with lustral water while words of benediction are said over it, sanctifying the fire to Brigid. The celebrant then stands before the candles to be distributed and proclaims a blessing over them, likewise sprinkling them three times with lustral water. They are then distributed to all in attendance. The celebrant lights their candle from the central fire or candle, and then lights another's, who then lights another's, and so forth.

During the fire blessing, the person taking on the part of Brigid and any attendants to her will have exited the house or area in preparation for her ceremonial entry. If resources allow for a more elaborate rite, she and her entourage may not have been present at all at the beginning, and their arrival should be coordinated to occur with great solemnity at this part of the ceremony.

Brigid arrives in beautiful array, carrying the rushes which will be used for making the Brigid's Crosses and a long unlit taper candle or lantern in hand. Those assembled should stand at ready attention at her arrival. The celebrant goes to the door of the home or entrance of the grove area, and the call and response begins. Brigid herself, or one of her attendants, knocks and proclaims from outside, with the celebrant answering from within.

After the third call and response, the celebrant opens the door and all present inside kneel or drop to one knee in welcome reverence, hailing Brigid. The celebrant genuflects before her, then lights her candle from their own. The celebrant then leads Brigid in a slow procession to the altar amidst the kneeling attendants. Appropriate, beautiful music may greatly amplify the tender solemnity of the moment. Reaching the altar, Brigid lays the rushes upon it or on a prepared table nearby. She then takes her seat in a special throne or chair set aside just for her for the ceremony. A *deasghnáth an neimhidh* then follows, offered specifically to Brigid.

After the offering proper and at the time for feasting or divination, a proper evening meal should be served. The rushes are allotted to each person and laid at their place at table; their dinner plates will be placed atop their share of rushes. There is a proper thanksgiving to Brigid prayed before the meal and after it.

Dinner being finished, all present then begin making their Brigid's Crosses, after which they set out their crosses and strips of cloth or clothing for Brigid to bless through the night. If the great tradition of a procession with the *Brídeóg* is to be observed the following day, the Brídeóg is also prepared at this time, and laid in an adorned bed ornamented with rushes, flowers or other such ameliorations until the next day's festivities.

The next day, in areas where possible, a grand and merry procession takes place with the *Brídeóg* carried and led by her attendants, bringing blessing and good fortune to all she passes by and driving out the cold of winter. The procession should conclude with another *deasghnáth an neimhidh* celebrated in the same manner as the night before, beginning with the enthronement of the *Brídeóg* before the altar or in another prominent spot to be offered to, and proceeding from the point in the rite where the offering proper begins.

A midday or afternoon meal may take place as a festive occasion at its proper point after the offering, along with divination for the rest of the winter season. It is said that a cloudy or stormy Imbolc tells of a short winter, for such weather prevents the Cailleach from collecting more wood for a long winter, while a clear day portends a protracted season of cold since that allows her to go out and collect enough to last it.

After the meal, the usual thanksgivings and éiric prayers are offered, and the rite is ended. The Brigid's Crosses should adorn a prominent place in the home until next Imbolc, when the old one may either be stored elsewhere in the house or burned in the Imbolc fire. The *Brídeóg* effigy should be treated with great respect. It may serve as a focal point for offerings and devotions to Brigid until the next Imbolc, when it may respectfully be burned in the Imbolc fire. Some may also preserve the *Brídeóg* but only until the Samhain of that year, to emphasize the tradition which views Brigid and Aongus as governing the light and warm half of the year, but relinquishing that governance to the Cailleach at Samhain. If preservation of the *Brídeóg* is not an option, in any case, it should be disposed of with due honor either by burial or fire, accompanying an offering to Brigid and divination to ascertain her ascent to the disposal.

Imbolc

Kindling is prepared for a suitably large bonfire outdoors. Due to the possibility of extreme cold, the fire for this festival may be kindled indoors. In that case, it should be lit from a candle of substantial size or distinction, or a triple branched candle to distinguish it in appearance and dignity.

Candles are prepared which, after their blessing, will be distributed to all present. They should be in a basket or collected altogether in some place for the beginning of the Rite, though not upon any harrow.

Croitheadh uisce naofa ~ Sprinkling of lustral water
As usual.

Lasadh agus naomhú na tine ~ Lighting and blessing of the fire

Ó Bhríd a Bhandia an-Bhuach,

Fíor-Sholas, a shoilsíonn na saolta

Fear (*celebrant sprinkles fire thrice with lustral water*) do bheannacht ar an tine seo,

agus naomhaigh í leis an solas do bhua;

mar a scaoileann an solas seo diamhracht oíchí le tine fheicseanach fhorloiscthe,

deonaigh dúinn ár meabhair a lonraíodh le tine neamhfheicseanach, sin é, an spéirghealach d'Inspreagtha,

go rabhaimid saor ón dhaille gach neamheolais;

agus ár súile intinne glanadh, ionas go haiththnímid le ceart, labhraímid an fhírinne, agus déanaimid go n-onóir.

Naomhú agus dáileamh na gcoinnle ~ Blessing and distribution of candles

The celebrant now stands before the collected candles.

Ó Bhríd a Bhandia an-Bhuach,
a soilsíonn, a leigheasann, agus a ngaibhníonn do thine,
le do cheird a ndearna tú an leacht seo
as obair na mbeach chun teinne céarach,
chun tine ar an bhfuaraíocht is solas sa dorchadas a bhreith;
a gcuir aithne ar do bhanóglaigh
buantine lasartha romhat a choimeád;
fear go mánla rath do bheannachta (*sprinkle candles thrice with lustral water*)
ar na choinnle seo,
ar chaoi go dtabharfaidís solas seachtrach,
sa chaoi is go saighneála an solas do Shoilsithe as do dhán inár gcinn.

The candles are distributed. The celebrant lights their candle from the central Fire, then lights another's candle, and so on.

Imbolc

Kindling is prepared for a suitably large bonfire outdoors. Due to the possibility of extreme cold, the fire for this festival may be kindled indoors. In that case, it should be lit from a candle of substantial size or distinction, or a triple branched candle to distinguish it in appearance and dignity.

Candles are prepared which, after their blessing, will be distributed to all present. They should be in a basket or collected altogether in some place for the beginning of the Rite, though not upon any harrow.

Croitheadh uisce naofa ~ Sprinkling of lustral water

As usual.

Lasadh agus naomhú na tine ~ Lighting and blessing of the fire

O Most-Glorious Goddess Brigid,
true light, who enlightens the worlds,
pour forth (*celebrant sprinkles fire thrice with lustral water*) your blessing upon this fire,
and hallow it with the light of your virtue;
grant, that just as this light kindled by visible fire dispels the darkness of night,
so our minds illumined by that invisible fire which is the brightness
of your Inspiration,
may be free from the blindness of every ignorance;
that our mind's eye being made pure, we may perceive rightly, speak the truth,
and act honorably.[6]

Naomhú agus dáileamh na gcoinnle ~ Blessing and distribution of candles

The celebrant now stands before the collected candles.

O Most-Glorious Goddess Brigid,
whose fire enlightens, heals and forges,
by your crafting knowledge you did cause this liquid
to come to wax by the work of bees,
to bear fire in the cold and light in the darkness;
who did command your handmaidens
to keep a perpetual fire burning before you;
graciously pour forth the virtue of your blessing (*sprinkle candles thrice with lustral water*)
upon these candles,
that they may so afford external light, that by your gift the light
of your Illumination may blaze in our heads.[7]

The candles are distributed. The celebrant lights their candle from the central Fire, then lights another's candle, and so on.

Fáilte shollúnta Bhríde ~ Solemn Welcome of Brigid

Those assembled should now line the processional way from the entrance of the holy space to the altar. If the rite is conducted indoors or in a home, this arrangement ought to be followed as best as possible.

The person chosen to represent Brigid will have been outside the house or grove to this point. The person is dressed in elevated and beautiful garb. The person bears the reeds to be used to make crosses in one arm and a well-made long candle in the other. The candle is unlit.

The person knocks on the door (or, if outdoors, rings a bell thrice) and says:

Feacaigí bhur nglúine,
tugaigí oirmhidin,
agus ligigí Bríd isteach!

The knocking and this proclamation is done three times. Each time a bit louder and more commanding. After each time, the celebrant proclaims in response, also louder and more commanding each time:

Feacaigí bhur nglúine,
leathaigí rosc is croí,
agus ligigí Bríd isteach!

All assembled inside genuflect or fall to their knees and exclaim:

Tar isteach, tar isteach, tar isteach!
Tá céad fáilte romhat!

The person as Brigid then enters.
The celebrant genuflects before her, says to her:

Is é a beatha, is é a beatha, a Bhandia Uaisle!

The celebrant lights Brigid's candle from their own. The celebrant then leads Brigid in a slow procession to the harrow amidst those assembled who may remain kneeling.

The person then lays the rushes under the harrow (if possible) or in front of it. The person may then be seated in a special chair or throne for the rest of the rite, or may participate with the rest of the assembly as usual.

Fáilte shollúnta Bhríde ~ Solemn Welcome of Brigid

Those assembled should now line the processional way from the entrance of the holy space to the altar. If the rite is conducted indoors or in a home, this arrangement ought to be followed as best as possible.

The person chosen to represent Brigid will have been outside the house or grove to this point. The person is dressed in elevated and beautiful garb. The person bears the reeds to be used to make crosses in one arm and a well-made long candle in the other. The candle is unlit.

The person knocks on the door (or, if outdoors, rings a bell thrice) and says:

Bend your knees!
Give reverence,
and let Brigid in!

The knocking and this proclamation is done three times. Each time a bit louder and more commanding. After each time, the celebrant proclaims in response, also louder and more commanding each time:

Bend your knees,
open wide both eye and heart,
and let Brigid in!

All assembled inside genuflect or fall to their knees and exclaim:

Come in, come in, come in!
You are a hundred times welcome!

The person as Brigid then enters.
The celebrant genuflects before her, says to her:

Welcome, welcome, the Noble Goddess!

The celebrant lights Brigid's candle from their own. The celebrant then leads Brigid in a slow procession to the harrow amidst those assembled who may remain kneeling.

The person then lays the rushes under the harrow (if possible) or in front of it. The person may then be seated in a special chair or throne for the rest of the rite, or may participate with the rest of the assembly as usual.

Íobairt do Bhríde ~ Offering to Brigid

Celebrant spreads lustral water over their hands and then dabs forehead, mouth, and heart with the water, saying:

A Bhandia ionúine, toirbhrím mé féin duit idir anam agus chorp leis an íobairt seo.

A Shinsir a mhilse mo chroí, tagaigí i gcabhair orm, i gcruth go n-onóraímid an Soilseach go fiúntach, d'fhonn is go bhfaighimid a beannachtaí.

Celebrant takes offering and sets it on or just in front of/to the side of the harrow. It is not yet poured out. Celebrant raises hands and prays the following on behalf of themselves, their people, family and friends:

A Bhríde Bhandia an-Bhuach,
ofrálaimid na hurnaithe is íobairt seo
mar a d'ordaigh ár Sinsir romhainn
le sochar dár n-anam is gcoirp,
dár gcairde is ngaolta,
le neartú na nDéithe
agus le cóir na saolta.

Neart ár Sinsir, bí dár neart anois,
inniu agus gach oíche is lá atá le teacht.
Go stiúra tú
Go naomhaí tú
agus go gcosnaí tú
sinn, ár muintir, agus go háirithe mo Chlann (list personal family names)
agus mo chairde is mo ghaolta (list names of people you especially wish to pray for).

Go neartaí an íobairt seo thú
Go nglaca tú leis an íobairt seo ónár lámha
Chun ard-onóra s'agatsa.

The rest of the deasghnáth *follows as ordinary until the feast after the pouring-out of the offerings.*

Íobairt do Bhríde ~ Offering to Brigid
*Celebrant spreads lustral water over their hands and then dabs
forehead, mouth, and heart with the water, saying:*

O Beloved Goddess, I dedicate myself to you, soul and body,
with this offering.

O dearest Ancestors of my heart, come to my assistance, that we
may honor the Bright One worthily, so that we may receive her
blessings.

*Celebrant takes offering and sets it on or just in front of/to the side of
the harrow. It is not yet poured out. Celebrant raises hands and prays
the following on behalf of themselves, their people, family and friends:*

O Glorious Goddess Brigid,
we offer these prayers and this sacrifice
as our Ancestors before us ordained
for the benefit of our souls and bodies,
for our friends and family,
for your strengthening
and the right order of the worlds.

Strength of our Ancestors, be our strength now,
today and every night and day to come.
May you guide
May you bless
and may you protect
us, our people, and especially my Clan (*list personal family names*)
and my friends and my family (*list names of people you especially
with to pray for*).

May this offering strengthen you
May you accept this offering from our hands
to your high-honor.

The rest of the deasghnáth *follows as ordinary until the feast after the pouring-out of the offerings.*

Fleá ~ Feast

Now a proper feast should commence. If tables are set up, the rushes should first be distributed at each person's place at table. The plates of food are placed over them while dining.

Making of Brigid's Crosses, etc.

After the meal, the assembly now makes Brigid's Crosses, the strips of fabric that will be laid out as Brait Bríd, *and the* Brídeóg *is prepared if a procession for the next day or other devotional is planned.*

Setting Outside of Crosses, etc.

After all is ready, the Crosses, Brait *and vestments for the* Brídeóg *are set outside so that Brigid may bless them as she walks the worlds overnight.*

The Rites for Oíche Bhríde *are now complete and may now either be closed with the usual ending to the rite, beginning after the Fleá. Alternatively, one may see this rite as not concluding until after the next days rites if there is to be a procession with the Brídeóg, etc. In which case, the rite is left open, so to speak, recognizing the sacredness enduring through the night and continuing through the next day's procession, culminating in a* deasghnáth an neimhidh *after the procession, which then concludes as usual thereby completing the celebration of* Imbolc.

The rite is now finished.

Bealtaine
Apr 30 – May 1

The next festival, marking the beginning of the Celtic summer half of the year, is Bealtaine. The name of the day is sometimes Anglicized as Beltane, or simply called May Day. This high holy day is at the opposite axis of the year as Samhain, and therefore in many ways celebrates the opposite themes. While Samhain is a day recognizing and celebrating death and the passing away of things, Bealtaine is the joyous festival of new life, vitality and fecundity.

The celebration begins at sundown of April 30th, again paralleling Samhain. The hearth fires and other lights are put out so that they be rekindled from the main Bealtaine bonfire. Indeed, one proposed etymology of the name Bealtaine itself is *bright fire*. Some traditions hold the lighting of two great fires, between which the cattle are driven to bestow luck and fertility upon them. From this comes the Irish idiom *idir dhá tine Bhealtaine*, to be *between two Bealtaine fires*, meaning to be caught in a dilemma. The day is also often referred to as *Lá Buí Bealtaine*, the yellow day of Bealtaine, for in Ireland its arrival is marked by the blooming of yellow flowers, which are then used as festive decoration upon homes and the May Bush, the *crann Bhealtaine* (lit. "Bealtaine tree") which is a large branch or small tree decorated with ribbons, egg shells and other adornments and set outside the home for the occasion. The day is also called *Céadamhan*, from *Céad-shamh(ain)*, meaning *first of summer*, again a sort of response to the opposing Samhain with its conjectured meaning as *end of summer*.

This day may be sacred to many deities, in particular the Mórrigna, the great goddesses of the land, sovereignty and fertility. These are the powerful triple goddesses Badb, Macha and Mórrigan, the last of which is thought by many to be the same as the goddess Anu/Anann. These goddesses are well known for their ferocity in war, but it is good to understand this ferociousness as that of the mother bear who is both nurturing and murderously defensive of her cubs. So too are the Mórrigna, who, as both protectors and manifestations of the land itself and its people, are gracious to nurture and provide abundance to those who treat them and the land with due honor and respect, but also quick to destroy and cause havoc to those who take advantage of their largess, who desecrate the land, or spread deceit and dishonor in their realms. Among the Scottish Gaelic traditions, the day is additionally sacred to the goddess Brigid and the god Aongus, who together usher in the summer this day, taking their place and May Queen and King until Samhain.

The Bealtaine Rite

The ceremony for Bealtaine begins much the same way as Samhain, only rather than the proclamation of a dying year and birth of a new, we declare the death of winter and the happy arrival of summer. Just as at Samhain, all fires and electronic devices should, where safely applicable, be extinguished and turned off as an echo of the ancient practice of putting out all other fires so that the hearths may be rekindled by the new fire. Many of the ritual actions from Samhain take place in opposite. Where one faces west, the direction towards the land of promise whither go the dead, in the Samhain rite now we face east, towards the rising sun and rebirth, the promise of a new beginning and the tenacious thriving of life. Where at Samhain we walked nine times counterclockwise around the grove symbolic of the manner of the Otherworld and the dead, now we walk twelve times clockwise, representing completion and the direction of the living, of growth and good fortune. A centuries-old poem is recited while these circumambulations around the growing fire are made, asking for Anann's (the Mórrigan's) blessing upon the fire, upon the people gathered and their families, their actions, animals and land.

After this, Anann and the Dagda are solemnly invoked, along with all the gods. The rest of the rite is then the usual *deasghnáth an neimhidh*, save for a special blessing after the time for divination and feasting. Here, if two fires are lit, the people and animals present walk between them while the celebrant proclaims the usual words of blessing over them. If two fires are not lit, it is ideal to have two people take two brands lit from the fire and stand so as to allow the people and animals to pass between them in similar manner. After the rite is complete and the fire has burned low, it is tradition to jump over the embers for the blessing of fertility and abundance in the year to come.

The next morning, it is a longstanding tradition to rise early and wash one's face with the morning dew. This will bestow health and beauty for the next year. Other traditions include the prohibition of lending butter or having butter taken from one's home on this day, for it signifies that the butter (and, symbolically, the abundance of one's home) will be stolen from it for the year. Additionally, no laborious work is to be done on this day.

There is the tradition in some parts, likely of British or Scandinavian origin, to crown a May Queen this day and erect the May Pole with dancing and festivities. One may choose to incorporate such traditions at will, and in a spiritual context, it would be well to elevate these actions within the context of a *deasghnáth an neimhidh* similar to the procession and meal on Imbolc with the *Brídeóg*. For example, the celebration may begin with the sprinkling of the festival area with lustral water, followed by the lighting of a large candle or fire. The blessing from the night before with its accompanying circumambulations may be repeated, though without the proclamation of the winter's death and new fire, for this has already happened the prior evening. Then, after the invocations of Anann and the Dagda, the May Queen might enter and be crowned, and the festivities of the May Pole take place, being symbolic of the two great divinities respectively. After some time, the May Queen may take a place of honor in the space, preferably next the May Pole, and the offering portion of the ceremony take place. After this, a festive meal should take place, after which the usual thanksgiving and éiric follow, and the closing of the ceremony.

Bealtaine

Croitheadh uisce naofa ~ Sprinkling of lustral water
As usual.

Lasadh na tine Bhealtaine ~ Lighting of the Bealtaine fire

The kindling for a suitably large fire is prepared. Shortly before sunset, all lights are extinguished, all electronics are powered off and, if possible, unplugged. At sunset the celebrant declares, facing east:

Fuair an geimhreadh bás, agus tá an samhradh ar baraíd teacht.
Agus táimid anseo inár seasamh idir ann is as
idir inné is amárach
idir breith is bás
idir talamh, muir, is neamh
idir an saol seo, an saol eile, is an saol thíos.

The celebrant or other attendant now lights the Bealtaine fire, preferably from flint or friction:

Ón am gan thús, ón seanaithinne a d›adhain an cruinne, tógaimis den Sheantine agus adhnaimis an samhradh.

The fire is lit. Celebrant and others stand in the east, facing center & then walk 12 times clockwise about the center, slowly saying each stanza for each circumambulation. After every 3 circles, stand in east for a moment of reflection and thanks while the celebrant casts three sprinkles of lustral water on the growing fire:

Bealtaine

Croitheadh uisce naofa ~ Sprinkling of lustral water
As usual.

Lasadh na tine Bhealtaine ~ Lighting of the Bealtaine fire

The kindling for a suitably large fire is prepared. Shortly before sunset, all lights are extinguished, all electronics are powered off and, if possible, unplugged. At sunset the celebrant declares, facing east:

The winter has died, and the summer about to arrive.
And here we stand between here and there
between yesterday and tomorrow
between birth and death
between earth, sea, and sky
between this world, the otherworld, and the underworld.

The celebrant or other attendant now lights the Bealtaine fire, preferably from flint or friction:

From the time without beginning, from the ancient spark which ignited the universe, let us take of the primordial fire and kindle the summer.

The fire is lit. Celebrant and others stand in the east, facing center & then walk 12 times clockwise about the center, slowly saying each stanza for each circumambulation. After every 3 circles, stand in east for a moment of reflection and thanks while the celebrant casts three sprinkles of lustral water on the growing fire:

1. Naomhaigh, a Thréadhacht fhíor nach gann,
Sinn féin, ár gcairde agus ár ngaolta.
Ar clár cumhra na raoin, ar cróicín caoin na binne.
Ar clár cumhra na raoin, ar cróicín caoin na binne.

2. Gach ní inár dtithe, nó 'tá inár seilbh,
Gach buar is barr, gach táin is ioth,
Ó Oíche Shamhna chun Oíche Bhealtaine,
Biseach maith, agus beannacht mhacánta,
Ó mhuir go muir, agus bun gach abhann,
Ó thonn go tonn, agus bonn gach steille.

3. Trí Ríon a gabhail seilbh ar gach ní inár stór,
An Thréadhacht dhearbh don ár ndíon le cóir;
Ó ár n-anamacha riar,
Is díon ár gciallaigh faoin sciath do bhua,
Díon ár gciallaigh faoin sciath do bhua.
Beannaigh gach ní, agus gach aon, atá sa neimheadh seo;

4. Cuir Sleá an Bhua inár lámha le bua flaithis,
Go n-am a bhfeicimid Tír Tairngire,
Go n-am a bhfeicimid Tír Tairngire.
Tráth tréigeann buar an buabhall bhó,
Tráth tréigeann caoirigh an caorach cró,
Tráth éiríonn gabhair ar binn an cheo,
Go dtreoraí an Thréadhacht trí thriall an-chortha,
Ó go dtreoraí an Thréadhacht trí thriall an-chortha.

5. An Té a bhfuair bua ar na Fomhóraigh ar dtús,
éist is friotháil orainn nuair a bhfeacaimid ár nglúine,
Anocht anocht an oíche seo anocht,
i do láthair a Bhandia Bua,
i do láthair a Bhandia Bua.

6. A Anann, a Mháthair na nDéithe,
Naomhaigh an uail is an crodh-lao;
Ná lig fuath nó foirne i ngar dúinn,
Fuadaigh orainn dóigheanna na ndaoithe.

1. Bless, O Threefold true and bountiful,
ourselves, our friends and our families.
On the fragrant plain, on the fair mountain home,
On the fragrant plain, on the fair mountain home.

2. Everything within our dwellings or in our possession,
All kine and crops, all flocks and corn,
From Samhain Eve to Bealtaine Eve,
With goodly progress and gentle blessing,
From sea to sea, and every river mouth,
From wave to wave, and base of waterfall.

3. Be the Three Queens taking possession of all to us belonging,
Be the sure Threefold Divinity protecting us in truth;
Oh! satisfy our souls,
And shield our loved ones beneath the shield of your power,
Shield our loved ones beneath the shield of your power.
Bless everything and every one, in this grove;

4. Place the Spear of Victory in our hands with the power of
sovereignty,
Till we see the Land of Promise,
Till we see the Land of Promise,
What time the kine shall forsake the stalls,
What time the sheep shall forsake the folds,
What time the goats shall ascend to the mount of mist,
May the tending of the Threefold follow them,
May the tending of the Threefold follow them.

5. You who did win victory over the Fomorians at the beginning,
Listen and attend us as we bend the knee to you,
Tonight tonight this night tonight,
In your presence, O Goddess of Victory,
In your presence, O Goddess of Victory.

6. Anann, O mother of the Gods,
Bless our flocks and bearing kine;
Hate nor troop let not come near us,
Drive from us the ways of the ignorant.

7. Coinnigh do shúil gach Luan is Máirt,
Ar crodh-lao is ar agha dára;
Iomchair linn ó bhinn go sáile,
Tionóil féin an tréad is an uail.

8. Gach Céadaoin agus Déardaoin bí leo,
Bíodh do lámh chaoin a choíche ina gcor;
Ionghair buar don bhuabhall bhó,
Ionghair caoirigh don chaorach cró.

9. Gach Aoine bí, a Bhandia, ar a gceann,
Treoraigh caoirigh as aghaidh na mbeann,
Lena n-uainín bheaga ina ndiaidh,
Timpeallaigh iad le timpeallacht Dhéithe.

10. Gach Satharn bí leo mar chách,
Tabhair gabhair isteach lena n-uail,
Gach meann is minseach go taobh sáile,
Is Leac an Aegir go h-ard,
Le biolair uaine suas a barr.

11. Treoir na Tréadhacht dár ndíon i gach cás,
Treoir an Daghda leis a lorga is a choire,
Solas na Bríde leis a lasair soilsithe,
Treoir Dian Céacht, Lia na sláinte,
Is Lugh Ildánach, Rí an flaithis.
Is gach Déithe eile a n-adhraimid agus a n-onóraímid anocht.

12. Beannaigh sinn féin agus ár gclann,
Beannaigh gach cré a thig ónar leasrach,
Beannaigh na Sinsir a bhfuil a sloinne orainn,
Beannaigh, a Bhandia, an té a rug óna broinn.

7. Keep your eye every Monday and Tuesday
On the bearing kine and the pairing queys;
Accompany us from hill to sea,
Gather yourself the sheep and their progeny.

8. Every Wednesday and Thursday be with them,
Be your gracious hand always about them;
Tend the cows down to their stalls,
Tend the sheep down to their folds!

9. Every Friday be you, O Goddess, at their head,
Lead the sheep from the face of the peaks,
With their innocent little lambs following them,
Encompass them with the Gods' encompassing.

10. Every Saturday be likewise with them,
Bring the goats in with their young,
Every kid and goat to the sea side,
And from the Rock of Aeglr on high,
With tresses green about its summit.

11. The strength of the Threefold be our shield in distress,
The strength of the Dagda, with his club and his cauldron,
The Light of Brigid with her illuminating flame,
The strength of Dian Céacht, Physician of health,
And of Lugh Many-skilled, the King of the sovereignty.
And of every other God whom we worship and honor tonight.

12. Bless ourselves and our children/clan,
Bless every one who shall come from our loins,
Bless the the Ancestors whose name we bear,
Bless, O Goddess, her from whose womb we came.

Celebrant and all stop and, standing in the east facing the fire, proclaim:

Gach naofacht, beannacht agus bua,
Bí ag faomhadh linn gach am is gach uair,
In ainm na Tréadhachta Bhandé Naofa,
na Morrígana, Anainn buaine.

Beil Tine bí dár díon anuas,

Celebrant prostrates and kisses the earth

Beil Tine bí dár díon suas,

Celebrant lifts hands aloft

Beil Tine bí dár díon máguaird,

Celebrant reaches toward fire with right hand, then kisses right fingers, then extends them to all while slowly turning clockwise

Gabhail naofacht Bealtaine uainn,
Gabhail naofacht Bealtaine uainn.

Celebrant and all stop and, standing in the east facing the fire, proclaim:

Every holiness, blessing and power,
Be yielded to us every time and every hour,
In the name of the Holy Threefold Goddess,
the Morrigan, Anann everlasting.

Be the Bel Fire to shield us downward,

Celebrant prostrates and kisses the earth

Be the Bel Fire to shield us upward,

Celebrant lifts hands aloft

Be the Bel Fire to shield us all around,

Celebrant reaches toward fire with right hand, then kisses right fingers, then extends them to all while slowly turning clockwise

Accepting our Beltane blessing from us,
Accepting our Beltane blessing from us.[8]

Achaní ar na Déithe ~ Invocation of the Gods

Anann

A Anann
A Ollmháthair
A Bhanríon na Bealtaine

A bheireann bua thar an geimhreadh mharbhántachta
A chuir fás faoin fásra foinn, agus an tine athbheochta as an fuaire,
Cuir fás fúinn fosta, agus bí linn cois tine seo.

An Dagda

A Dhagda
A Eochaid Ollathair
A Ruadh Ro-Fessa

A dtugann do Lorga Mhór beatha is bás,
Agus nach n-imíonn a choire aon duine neamhshásta as,
Bí linn cois tine seo.

Na Déithe uile

Gairim ar na Déithe Uile Ró-Naofa,
Na Déithe Buacha na Talún, Mara, is Neimhe,
Na Déithe ár Sinsear ó thosach aimsire.
Go naomhaí sibh linn agus bígí linn anocht.

The rite then follows as the ordinary deasghnáth, save that at the communal blessing, two individuals take two brands lit from the Bealtaine fire. All present then walk between the brands while the celebrant proclaims over them the Neart Fiaigh Duibh...

Rites for Bealtaine Day

On May Day itself it is custom to rise early and wash one's face with the morning dew. The face is left to dry by air, not by towel or any other means.

It is also fitting to mark the day with fairs, festivities, much music and feasting.

Achaíní ar na Déithe ~ Invocation of the Gods

Anann

O Anann
O Allmother
O Queen of the May

Who claims victory over the winter of stagnation
Who makes the plants of the earth to grow, and the fire of new
life from the cold,
Make us to grow too, and be with us beside this fire.

An Dagda

A Dhagda
A Eochaid Ollathair
A Ruadh Ro-Fessa

Whose mighty club bestows life and death
and from whose cauldron goes none away unsatisfied,
be with us beside this fire.

All the Gods

I call upon all the Most-Holy Gods,
The Mighty Gods of Earth, Sea, and Sky,
The Gods of our Ancestors from the beginning of time,
may you bless us and be with us tonight.

*The rite then follows as the ordinary deasghnáth, save that at the
communal blessing, two individuals take two brands lit from the
Bealtaine fire. All present then walk between the brands while the
celebrant proclaims over them the* Neart Fiaigh Duibh...

Rites for Bealtaine Day

On May Day itself it is custom to rise early and wash one's face with the morning dew. The face is left to dry by air, not by towel or any other means.

It is also fitting to mark the day with fairs, festivities, much music and feasting.

Lughnasadh
July 31 – Aug 1

The latter festival of the summer half of the year is Lughnasadh (modern spelling *Lúnasa*). The name of this holy day comes from the shining God Lugh and the word *nasadh* which means *assembly*. *The assembly of Lugh*. The day is foremost the ancestral harvest festival, marking the merry occasion when the fields are first fruits of the crops are ready to be reaped.

As the name of the festival makes clear, the day is sacred to the God Lugh. Lugh is preeminent as one of those among the gods who serves as high king. He is grandson of Balor of the Evil Eye, the titanic Fomorian who in primordial times cast blight and death on the land of Ireland and to the Tuatha Dé Danann with a mere stare from his wicked eye. Balor's daughter Ethniu joined with Cian of the Tuatha Dé Danann, and bore a son— Lugh. It was prophesied that Balor's downfall would come from his daughter's child, and so Cian gave the child to Taillte who raised the child as her foster-son.

Lugh grew to become the most variously skilled among the Gods. When asked what his ability was, he demonstrated his excellence in all feats, and so in the course of the lore assumed the position as high king of the Gods, leading them in battle against the Fomorians, slaying his grandfather Balor, and bringing victory to the Tuatha Dé Danann. It is in the course of that same lore, however, that we learn of how his foster-mother Taillte cleared the plains of Ireland so that they may be fit for agriculture and, having done so, she died of exhaustion. Stricken with grief at the loss, Lugh solemnly instituted this harvest festival as "funeral games" to her honor.

While little beyond this is said in the surviving lore about Taillte, her very name suggests an identification with the earth itself. Indeed, tailte is simply a plural grammatical form of the Modern Irish word for "earth" or "ground" itself. Therefore, given the connection of the festival to the gleaning of the earth's first fruits, we may do well to conjecture in Taillte a sort of earth or agricultural goddess with spiritual, motherly connections to the rich soil which nourishes us with its yield. Another theory proposes that the name originates from the location where the festival had its central celebration, Tailtin (English "Teltown"), a townland in County Meath, Ireland. Surviving resources are unclear if the place is named for Taillte, or if Taillte was idealized later as part of lore springing up from a festival already practiced at the place. The care given to her deliberate mentioning in the oldest surviving lore, and her preeminent position as foster-mother of so great and prominent a deity as Lugh, along with linguistic connection to the very word for "earth" and "soil" itself (and cognates to other linguistically and religiously related deities such as the Roman Earth Goddess Tellus), all strongly suggest her ancestral veneration as indeed an earth or agricultural goddess.

The Lughnasadh rite

The rite here is presented differently from the other festivals, in that it does not necessitate the context of a *deasghnáth* in a grove, but rather provides an opening blessing to the harvest festival and games, as well as a solemn invocation of Lugh and Taillte. To be sure, one should offer a proper *deasghnáth* as well, using the opening blessing after the lighting of the fire, and the solemn invocations of Lugh and Taillte at the ordinary point when the Gods are invoked. The rite is written without that framework so as to highly recommend the revival of marking this sacred time with games and feasting, as it is for that purpose that Lugh is said to have instituted the festival, and by engaging in such we fulfill that ancestral and divine memorial. That is, first and foremost, our Lughnasadh offering.

Lughnasadh

Beannú na gcluichí is féile ~ Blessing of the games and festival

Adhraimid thú, a Lugh, agus onóraímid do Mháthair Altrama, Taillte Tíre Talún.
Tagaimid romhat inniu in ómós na té a rinne na gort glan.
Go méadaí tú gach aon neach ar an saol seo agus an saol eile a dhéanas cuimhneamh ar do Bhanaltra Mhór.

Solemn invocation of Lugh and Tailte (*within the rite proper, after the invocation of Manannán*)

Lugh

Fáilte romhat a Lugh! A Rí! Ildánach! Lámhfhada! Fáilte!
Ó Rí is Tiarna lonrach geal,
cosantóir, cuinge is ceann
as na tonnta ardaithe le soilsiú mar an ghrian

As Findias is faide trasna na tonnta ón Uscias bith-bhorb a ghaibhnigh an ga d'oirbhirt
ina aghaidh ní féidir leis aon áibhirseoir dréim.
Gairimid agus onóraimid thú ar an tórraimh seo,
Ó Té a dtugann a bhrí beatha do gach aon neach faoin ghréine
a dealraíonn bláth ar ainmhí is duine
a dtugann a sholas fónta matihe na talún,
An Talamh, a Talamh, a Talamh dhil is fhial!

Ó Lugh, Ceann Croic solasmhar Tiarna is Rí,
bí linn is iaigí linn anois nuair a n-onóraimid is a ngairimid do Mháthair Altrama dhílis, ina cuimhne a mbunaigh tú an fheis ársa seo:

Lughnasadh

Beannú na gcluichí is féile ~ Blessing of the games and festival

We adore you, Lugh, and we honor your Foster Mother, Taillte of Land and Earth.
We come before you today in homage of she who cleared the fields.
May you prosper every one in this world and the Otherworld who commemorates your great Foster-mother.

Solemn invocation of Lugh and Tailte (*within the rite proper, after the invocation of Manannán*)

Lugh

Hail Lugh! King! Many-skilled! Long-arm! Hail!
O shining lord and king,
defender, protector and chieftain
raised from the waves to shine like the sun

From far-away Findias over the sea of ever-fierce Uscias
smithied the spear you wield against which no adversary can contend.
We hail and honor you on this harvest day,
O you whose vigor brings life to all creatures
Who shines down abundance on animal and man
Whose nourishing light brings forth the fruits of the earth,
The Earth, the Earth, bountiful dearest Earth!

O Lugh, shining chieftain lord and king,
be with us and join us now as we honor and invoke your beloved Foster-Mother, in whose memory you instituted this ancient feast:

Taillte

Fáilte romhat, a Taillte! Tír, Talamh, a Mháthair Altrama Lugh! Fáilte!
Ó Taillte, ní Mhag Mhor, Ríon na bhFear Bolg,

"Is í an Tailltese ba bhean Echach mic Eirc, Rí na hÉireann.
Cian mac Déin Chécht, Scál Balb ainm eile dó,
a mac di ar altram, mar a bhí Lugh. Eithne ní Bhalair Bailcbeimnig a máthairse.
Chuaigh Taillte d'éag i dTailltín, is cheangail a hainm de.
Déantar a cluiche gach bhliain agus a caoin di le Lugh,
le geasa is geallta gaisce,
coicís riamh Lughnasadh agus coicís iaramh Lughnasadh."

De réir an bhunaithe Lugh agus ár sinsear romhainn,
leis seo onóraíonn sinn thú leis an fhéile ró-fhéatach is shollúnta,

Ó Taillte, Tír, Talamh, a Mháthair Altrama Lugh!
Beirimid buíochas ónar gcroíthe duit as an bheatha, mhéith is bhláth a bhfearann tú.
Go bhfaightear ár n-íobairt is ár gcoimeád na féile ró-naofa is ársa seo agus go n-onóraí sí thú,
a Mháthair Altrama dhil, agus go gcothaí tú sinn le do rath ionas go mbeirimid beo ar an am seo arís.

The rite is finished.

Taillte

Hail Taillte! Land, Earth, Foster-Mother of Lugh! Hail!
O Taillte, daughter of Mag Mor, Queen of the Fir Bolg,

"That Taillte who was wife of Eochu son of Erc, King of Ireland.
Cian son of Dian Cecht, whose other name was Scal Balb, gave
to her his son Lugh in fosterage. Eithne daughter of Balar the
Strong-Smiter was indeed her mother.
Taillte died in Taillte, and so to it clung her name.
Her funerary games are made every year, and a keening for her,
by Lugh.
With *geasa* (sacred injunctions) and feats-of-arms,
a fortnight before Lughnasadh and a fortnight after."[9]

In accord with the institution of Lugh and our ancestors before
us, we hereby honor you with this most solemn and festive feast,

O Taillte, Land, Earth, Foster-Mother of Lugh!
We give heartfelt thanks for the richness and nourishment and
abundance you provide.
May our offering and our observance of this ancient most-holy
feast be received by you and honor you, dearest Foster-Mother,
and may you deign to sustain us
through your bounty that we may warrant to live to see this
time again.

The rite is finished.

Endnotes

1. Carmichael, Alexander. *Carmina Gadelica*. Vol. 1. T. and A. Constable, 1900. (6 - 11)
   The purification rite is inspired by one of the beautiful poems collected by Alexander Carmichael in his Carmina Gadelica. This is a wonderful assemblage of Gaelic poetry and lore gleaned by Carmichael from Gaelic-speaking Scotland between 1860 and 1909. Its content, much of it devotional and uniquely Gaelic in nature, yields much fruit for those looking for natively Celtic material to foster their own prayers and liturgies.

2. Gregory, Lady Augusta. *Gods and Fighting Men*. John Murray, 1904. (69)
   Lady Augusta Gregory was an instrumental writer and folklorist in the Irish Literary Revival. My translation of the Song of Amergin is largely based on her own, though I have taken lengths to make my Modern Irish translation reflect the Old Irish original as closely as possible, even using words of the same etymological root which preserves some of the obscurity of the original.

3. Best, R.I. *The Settling of the Manor of Tara*. Ériu. Vol. 4. Royal Irish Academy, 1910. (146)

4. Gwynn, Edward. *The Metrical Dindshenchas Part 3*. Royal Irish Academy Todd Lecture Series. Vol. 10. Hodges, Figgis, & Co., 1913 (292 - 293)

5. Gwynn, Edward. *The Metrical Dindshenchas Part 3*. Royal Irish Academy Todd Lecture Series. Vol. 10. Hodges, Figgis, & Co., 1913 (28 - 29)

These two passages are both found among the dindshenchas, collections of place-name lore providing the mythical and poetic origins for the names of places across Ireland. Here we have the dindshenchas for the Well of Connla and the Well of Segais, each having mythic connections to Shannon and Boann respectively.

6. *The Roman Missal for the use of the Laity.* P. Keating, Brown & Co., 1806 (550)

7. *The Roman Missal for the use of the Laity.* P. Keating, Brown & Co., 1806 (549)
   These beautiful passages consecrating the lights used for Imbolc *are from the traditional Roman Missal, the text used for the liturgy of the Roman Catholic Mass until its use was largely superseded by a New Order of Mass promulgated after the Second Vatican Council. Whether under the guise of St Brigid's Day, or the traditional Roman Catholic festival of Candlemas or the Purification of the Blessed Virgin Mary, there is no denying the inherent, sacred and indigenously pagan nature of these ceremonies which seek to bring a holiness of light and fire into the cold of winter and herald the first hints of spring. These prayers, even though Catholic in nature, well embody the hidden hope and mystery of this ancient festival.*

8. Carmichael, Alexander. *Carmina Gadelica.* Vol. 1. T. and A. Constable, 1900. (182 - 189)
   Once again, Carmichael nourishes us with rich Gaelic fare in this Beltane blessing. *The original, of course, references the Christian Trinity in its invocations of "the Threefold" divinity, etc. This is no obstacle for our adaptation, however, as we honor our own ancient Threefold Goddess on this day.*

9. R.A.S. Macalister. *Lebor Gabála Érenn: Book of the Taking of Ireland.* Vol. 4. Irish Texts Society, 1941. (§59)

This passage is from what is elsewhere also known as the Book of Invasions. *In a few short sentences we are given a brief glimpse of what may be surviving lore as to the origin of the Lughnasadh festival. We hear of* Taillte, *foster-mother of* Lugh, *who perishes of exhaustion after clearing the plains of Ireland for cultivation.* Lugh *then institutes the festival of Lughnasadh as commemoratory funeral games in her honor.*

Select Bibliography

Best, R.I. *The Settling of the Manor of Tara*. Ériu. Vol. 4. Royal Irish Academy, 1910.

Carmichael, Alexander. *Carmina Gadelica*. Vol. 1. T. and A. Constable, 1900.

Danaher, Kevin. *The Year in Ireland*. The Mercier Press, 1972.

Gregory, Lady Augusta. *Gods and Fighting Men*. John Murray, 1904.

Gwynn, Edward. *The Metrical Dindshenchas Part 3*. Royal Irish Academy Todd Lecture Series. Vol. 10. Hodges, Figgis, & Co., 1913.

Ó Laoghaire, Diarmuid, S.J. Ár bPaidreacha Dúchais. 6th ed. Foilseacháin Ábhair Spioradálta, 1990.

R.A.S. Macalister. *Lebor Gabála Érenn: Book of the Taking of Ireland*. Vol. 4. Irish Texts Society, 1941.

The Roman Missal for the use of the Laity. P. Keating, Brown & Co., 1806.

About the Author

John McLoughlin lives and writes on the brisk, beautiful shores of Lake Superior. As a devotee and lover of traditional Irish spirituality, lore, and language, he is passionate about sharing these ancestral ways with others, providing strong foundations for seekers new to the path, as well as deep and enriching material for the experienced wayfarer.

You may also like

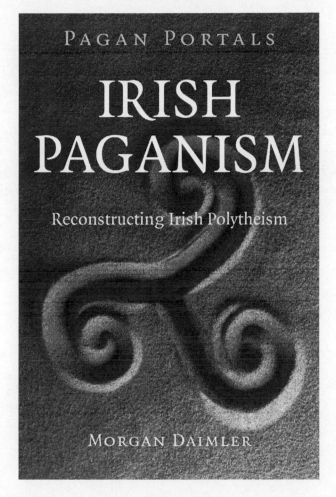

PAGAN PORTALS

IRISH PAGANISM

Reconstructing Irish Polytheism

MORGAN DAIMLER

Irish Paganism - Reconstructing Irish Polytheism
by Morgan Daimler

*Reconstructing the beliefs and practices of pre-Christian Irish
Paganism for the modern world*

978-1-78535-145-7 (Paperback)
978-1-78535-146-4 (e-book)

Readers of ebooks can buy or view any of these bestsellers by clicking on the live link in the title. Most titles are published in paperback and as an ebook. Paperbacks are available in traditional bookshops. Both print and ebook formats are available online.

Find more titles and sign up to our readers' newsletter
http://www.Johnhuntpublishing.com/paganism

For video content, author interviews and more, please subscribe to our YouTube channel.

MoonBooksPublishing

Follow us on social media for book news, promotions and more:

Facebook: Moon Books Publishing

Instagram: @moonbooksjhp

Twitter: @MoonBooksJHP

Tik Tok: @moonbooksjhp